LITERARY WORKS BY 10 DOMINICAN WOMEN

LITERARY WORKS BY 10 DOMINICAN WOMEN

Kianny N. Antigua
Compilation and Edition

Kadiri J. Vaquer Fernández
Translation

Literary Works By 10 Dominican Women
Copyright © 2020 Kianny N. Antigua

Compilation and Edition: **Kianny N. Antigua**
    kiannyantigua@gmail.com

Translation from the Spanish: **Kadiri J. Vaquer Fernández**
    k.vaquer@gmail.com

Copy Editing: **Courtney Aucone**
    caaucone@gmail.com

Illustrator and Cover Designer: **Nathalie Rodríguez Sánchez**
    nathrodriguez@gmail.com
    Instagram@nathammer

DWA Press is an Imprint of Dominican Writers Assoc., a 501 (c)(3) non-profit literary arts organization founded in 2015 with the mission to support Dominican writers by providing them the tools and resources to become published authors.

All rights reserved.
No part of this book may be reproduced or transmitted in any form or by any means, electronic or mechanical, including photocopying, recording, or by an information storage and retrieval system—except by a reviewer who may quote brief passages in a review to be printed in a magazine or newspaper—without permission in writing from the holder of the copyright. Please do not participate in or encourage piracy of copyright materials in violation of the author's rights. Purchase only authorized editions.

ISBN: 978-1-7372467-3-2

DWA Press
An Imprint of the Dominican Writers Association, Inc.
www.dominicanwriters.com
Email: info@dominicanwriters.com

For our youth.

CONTENTS

Introduction..3

Translator's Note..5

Camila Henríquez Ureña..7
- «Daughter of the Sun» by Kianny N. Antigua
- Poems by Camila Henríquez Ureña: «Life and Freedom»
- «The Root»
- «Endless Voice»
- Camila Henríquez Ureña's Biography

Rhina Espaillat..17
- «Parallel Lines» by César Sánchez Beras
- Poems by Rhina Espaillat: «Stanzas: I Was Born in the First City...»
- «Fourteen Years Old»
- «Snowing»
- Rhina Espaillat's Biography

Mélida García..29
- «Unwavering Mélida» by Osiris Mosquea
- Short Story by Mélida García: «Of What Happened that Terrible Day When Time Decided to Demand Vindications»
- Mélida García's Biography

Osiris Mosquea..39
- «My Color» by José Acosta
- Poems by Osiris Mosquea: «In the Almost Island»
- «Immigrating Towards Whitman»
- «God, Where Were You When the Angel Lost Its Wings?»
- Osiris Mosquea's Biography

Josefina Báez..53
- «Matches» by Keiselim A. Montás
- Narrative Texts by Josefina Báez: «Micro-story 1»
- «Micro-story 2»
- «Ana and Anand»
- Josefina Báez's Biography

Aurora Arias..67
- «True History of a Tropical Night» by Néstor E. Rodríguez
- Short Story by Aurora Arias: «Driving Around»
- Aurora Arias' Biography

Yrene Santos...77
- «Yrene Santos López» by Carlos Aguasaco
- Poems by Yrene Santos: «The Woman»
- «Certainty»
- «3»
- «4»
- Yrene Santos' Biography

Marianela Medrano..89
- «Marianela Medrano: Sensibility and Resilience» by Aurora Arias
- Poem by Marianela Medrano: «Post-Generation X»
- Marianela Medrano's Biography

Sussy Santana..105
- «Shapes of a Kiss» by Rey Andújar
- Poems by Sussy Santana: «Paper Dolls»
- «Femicide»
- «Blessing»
- «Woman»
- Sussy Santana's Biography

Rosa Silverio..121
- «Rosa Silverio» by Frank Báez

- Poems by Rosa Silverio: «Crazier Than a Goat»
- «When a Voice Dies»
- «One Must Name This Sadness»
- Rosa Silverio's Biography

Collaborators' Biographies 133
- José Acosta
- Carlos Aguasaco
- Rey Andújar
- Aurora Arias
- Frank Báez
- Keiselim A. Montás
- Osiris Mosquea
- César Sánchez Beras
- Néstor E. Rodríguez

Compiler/Editor's and Translator's Biographies 137
- Kianny N. Antigua
- Kadiri J. Vaquer Fernández

INTRODUCTION

There is a huge gap in the literary study of Dominican women writers. It is equally concerning that our growing generations do not find—neither in books nor in the mega-world of social media—models of ink and light of these talented, brave and transgressive women. With this subjective publication and collaborations from good friends, excellent writers themselves, I unlock the door to the marvelous worlds of ten writers, *Literary Works by 10 Dominican Women*, to our history, a gate to our diaspora and our present. Many, many great women writers are missing and could have well been a part of this anthology, which is why it was such a difficult task to make this selection. All I can do now is apologize for this offense, and shield myself behind the problem of space and pragmatism. However, since my intention is to trigger your curiosity, to encourage scrutiny, I hope this project will instill a desire to read, to know.

Without further delay, it is my privilege to present to you a compilation of texts that vary in genre, time periods, literary trends, styles, motivations and topics; texts by women writers who, due to their talent, art, education, persistence, strength, love and respect for writing, have become pillars of our literature. Today, we remember and honor them; today, we study and celebrate them; tomorrow, young readers, you will be the homeland.

Kianny N. Antigua
Compiler and Editor

TRANSLATOR'S NOTE

After years of asking myself why I had not been exposed to more Dominican writers, of looking at graduate reading lists and feeling upset and discouraged by the lack of Puerto Rican and Dominican writers, I decided to translate this book. They say, "You can't be something you can't see." If we are missing representation from reading lists and classroom lessons, what does that say about our words, our experiences, and our cultures? That we are not writers? Poets? That we are inexistent? That our voices are expendable?

Some say translators are traitors. Others say translation is an impossible task, doomed to fail. It is important to understand that a translation is not meant to replicate the original, but rather to recreate, to reimagine the original. In the end, without translation, our reading alternatives would be highly limited and our islands continuously erased by academia and the market. The work of translation is much like a conversation in which the translator is constantly negotiating meaning, style, and form. When you're lucky, like I have been, you can engage in that conversation with the writers and discuss options, other versions, clarify images or regionalisms. These conversations tend to lead to a better understanding of the work and a deep sense of shared complicity.

By delving into this anthology filled with a polyphony of voices exploring freedom, exile, migration, longing, race, gender, death, violence, and rural and urban landscapes, I was reminded of the impact the diasporic experience has on our sense of self and identity. For months, I have traveled with these women. I have seen their hometowns, glimpsed at their childhood years, watched them wait at a train station, saw them board a bus and say goodbye. I have pictured the women they speak of, the violence they experienced, and the strong women they looked up to and became. At times, I felt so close to home as I sunk into their words. After all, I am also a Caribbean woman navigating the diaspora with my eyes and heart, facing the island while my feet struggle to take root on North American soil.

The process of translating this book has been, in many ways, a chance to bridge two islands that at times look like an archipelago. Ultimately, I hope that rather than a traitor, I have been a sister, a *comadre*.

Kadiri J. Vaquer Fernández

1. **CAMILA HENRÍQUEZ UREÑA**

Daughter of the Sun

To CAMILA HENRÍQUEZ UREÑA
By Kianny N. Antigua

> *To be born from the sun*
> *has its complexities*
> *all the planets revolve*
> *in the shadow of its light.*

Being born into a bourgeois family gives you the opportunity to choose: to choose what to eat, what to study, where to live, etc. For Camila Henríquez Ureña—whose father held a high-ranking political and governmental position, was a doctor and a lawyer, and whose mother was an innovative, enterprising and talented woman, characteristics rarely seen (rarely appreciated and rarely tolerated) in a woman of the time—these social advantages turned into both a virtue and a curse. A virtue because her parents' name, the same as her brothers', opened many doors for her (as well as her financial stability); a curse because, for many years, Camila's talent and contributions have been overshadowed, even ignored, due to her family's achievements.

Surely this situation was expected: Camila Henríquez Ureña never got married nor had children. "Single" and "childless" were not and, to date, are not the most admirable or respectable traits for a woman, even if that woman was a writer, a university professor and department chair at one of the most prestigious universities in the United States. Her work and contributions to the Cuban and Mexican education systems during her time as an advisor for the Ministerio de Educación in Havana, are equally commendable.

A woman who never got married nor had any children could not be a source of admiration in a world in which women are expected to stay in the kitchen. Even if her contributions and accomplishments had turned the doorknob on Latin-American education, Camila Henríquez Ureña was always seen as an incomplete woman. As if being single were a physical condition or a mental disadvantage, a handicap. As if giving birth certified a woman's intellectual and human ability.

> *A shadow in a society made of shadows,*
> *in which giving birth is the great*
> *and irrefutable answer.*

Jóvenes, we have to change the world! What makes a single man a bachelor and a single woman a failure? Nothing, nothing more than a patriarchal misconception, the one we carry on our shoulders like mountains (the one that keeps us from making the same salary as men, even when we are equally qualified and hold the same positions; the one that, even today, ties our daughters to the sink while their brothers are out playing in the street and doing "guy stuff;" the *machismo* that screams at us, both implicitly and explicitly, that we don't have the same abilities as men; that's why, instead of being called poet we are still called *poetisa*, instead of tailor, seamstress; and instead of bishops or Popes, ah, that's right, women are supposedly undeserving of such a high and pure rank… We—approximately 100,000 years after the Homo Sapiens, the Wise Man—we are still viewed and considered less in many aspects of our daily lives), *pero basta*, enough!

Camila Henríquez Ureña was a pillar of our education and literature, and if she was not acknowledged for her weight in gold before, today is the day to change that! Today is the moment to break away from the traditions and the misogynistic practices; to liberate us from such flawed convictions, so often confused for "customs," and to replace them by celebrating the compelling, creative force of our women writers, regardless of their marital or social status, whatever their skin color or the texture of their hair. Today, we will honor the eminence of women who, like Camila, are stars and suns with constellations of their own.

> *To be born from the sun*
> *has its complexities,*
> *but its virtue too:*
> *you shine,*
> *you shine perpetually!*

POEMS BY CAMILA HENRÍQUEZ UREÑA

Life and Freedom

This is my life, the one in the peaks,
surrounded by the fair breeze,
there where the last bird nests
and the dark is undone on the golden crests!
This is my freedom: T bear and smell the rose,
to cut the cold water the way my crazy hand knows,
to undress the tender woods,
to remove the sun's eternal glow!

The Root

Out in the countryside where the flowers dance full of grace
and the foliage's green sonata resonates.
Of my amphoras once filled with scents now there is no trace
for the colors overflow and fill the entire landscape.

While my feet are quick to reciprocate the earth's fervent
kiss in the same way the branches that caress my head do,
I recall the root covered by dust's deterrent
the ignored origin from where vital beauty breaks through.

The root is too like a loving mother who quietly
stows the fruit, hiding it underneath the dark mat
it stretches through the branches and elevates slowly
toward the light, that is the shade's slow task.

The outside layers can always be made new.
The leaves fall, the stems break, and the flowers' heads begin to wither
when the fruit simply waits for a hand to come and choose,
yet life does not disrupt its fragrance which never turns bitter.

And the plant will be reborn, if the attentive root
can sustain its deeply mysterious and fertile beat.
The root owns nothing, but bears everything
and through its veins runs the force that made the world complete.

My love, all of my blood is pouring out from the lesion,
drink up and rise your magnificent beauty to the sun!
I am the depth, a knot hidden in life's secret region,
a root stemming from where the dark eternity begun.

Endless Voice

Peace never begins without a bell or a dove…
It seems like the two made an agreement with the sun.

Silence is made of gold. The evening is made of glass
and through the cool trees travels a purity hard to surpass.
Far beyond, where dreams dwell, the river still shines brilliantly.
It separates pearls then escapes into infinity.

Solitude! Solitude! All is bright and without words.
Peace never begins without a bell or a bird…

Love lives far, too from here. Undisturbed and indifferent
the heart is like a book. It is neither sad nor content.
It is distracted by colors, winds, caresses and scents…
Nothing better than a lake full of immune sentiments.

Peace never begins without a bell or a dove.
It seems like eternity can be captured with a glove.

BIOGRAPHY

SALOMÉ CAMILA HENRÍQUEZ UREÑA [Santo Doming, April 9, 1894 – September 12, 1973]. Henríquez Ureña was an educator, essayist, literary critic, humanist, feminist and poet. She is considered one of the most illustrious Latin-American intellectuals of the 20th century. She lived in Cuba since she was 10 years old. By the time she was 22 she had completed a PhD in Philosophy, Letters and Pedagogy. Shortly after, she moved to Minnesota, USA, where she earned a master's degree in arts. She also studied at Columbia University and the Sorbonne, France. She was a professor at the University of Minnesota, Middlebury College and the University of Havana. Henríquez Ureña worked at the Fondo de Cultura, Mexico, and in Cuba where she presided the Sociedad Femenina Lyceum. In collaboration with her brother, she founded the Institución Hispano Cubana de Cultura . In addition, she was an advisor for the Ministerio de Educación. As a woman of her time period, she was not as renowned abroad as her brothers Pedro and Max. In the Dominican Republic, she was hidden beneath the shadow of her mother, the National Poet, Salomé Ureña de Henríquez. Nevertheless, intellectuals, students, and readers have come to recognize our formidable Camila for her immeasurable literary contributions.

The poems *"Vida y libertad," "La raíz"* and *"Voz inmensa"* were selected from *Obras y apuntes. Camila Henríquez Ureña. Tomo III & X* (BanReservas, 2014).

2. RHINA ESPAILLAT

Parallel Lines

To RHINA ESPAILLAT
By César Sánchez Beras

"Mommy, where are we going?" Little Rhina asked, and her question floated in the air during seconds that seemed like minutes.

"I don't know yet, *mi hija*," Dulce María replied. And she continued to walk in the same direction, just a bit faster now.

At her tender age, little Rhina had a feeling that something important was going on. She had been dressed up in Sunday clothes when it was only Tuesday; her hair was picked up and twisted into a bun that sat on top of her head, she did not like it because to her it looked like an onion and she was scared the other girls would make fun of her hairdo. She was wearing a beautiful pink dress and her shoes were shiny, pink patent leather. Her whole outfit confirmed that she was dressed for a trip. Homero would be waiting for them somewhere, but Rhina's mother hadn't had any time to even think about being reunited with her husband. They loved what they were leaving behind way too much. The broad streets with slow traffic in the mornings, the curious neighbors chatting about the news aloud and talking about the political issues in whispers and signs; the childhood friends, the aunts and nephews, the rivers and the trees, the park on Sunday afternoons, everything, absolutely everything, ripped out in the blink of an eye to be left in the past.

The flame trees along the streets in La Vega Real were nearly through the last days of spring and the black pods were starting to disfigure the flowers' flaming red, as if it were a warning from nature confirming the worst was yet to come.

Little Rhina smiled at the people walking by the old bus that would take her to the capital. She had her notepad, the one she never left behind, in which she drew *cayena* flowers and wrote down words that sounded beautiful to her.

"Perhaps someday I will become a poet," she would tell herself. Being a seamstress like her mother had its charm, being that she transformed pieces of fabric into elegant dresses. For young Rhina, becoming a poet was more or less the same, as it involved joining pieces of words to create dresses for different feelings. Her mother could hardly see the small stitches on the garments she made but Rhina wanted to see her name on book covers. On the way to the capital, Dulce stroked her daughter's hair and with her free hand, wiped her tears with her handkerchief, the one with her initials on it.

"Better times will come, *mi hija*," the mother said, but little Rhina did not understand her words and she continued to wave at people from the bus window. Dulce María was not too certain about what she had said either.

Nearly a decade ago, the same thing had happened on the other side of the world. It was almost like the universe was a coin with two identical sides. David, like many other emigrants, had left everything behind him to begin a journey with no return. Romania was a beautiful place to live, but life was short there. The day they set off, the sea was a promising postcard. The waves announced a turbulent trip, but the hope for a peaceful place exceeded the troubles of that choppy journey. Alfred would be born in New York. His mother always knew he was going to be an artist. He paid special attention to the shape of things. He was extremely sweet and quiet, as if the artist he would become were constantly erupting.

Fate's threads mysteriously intertwine and no one knows which gods tossed the dice to determine the other person's luck. The first time Rhina and Alfred exchanged looks they were at the wedding of some mutual friends. Alfred looked at her and drank up her laughter. He listened to her words and was lulled, thinking of ways he would sculpt the harmony that Rhina inspired in him. Suddenly, a doubt came to mind:

"What will her father think of an emigrant descendant of Jews?" He asked himself, but by then it was too late to be scared.

The next time they saw each other it was clear there was no going back. When Alfred looked at Rhina, he saw all the lines in the universe converge on her Caribbean skin, her curly hair and her bewitching laughter. She was, from every angle, the marble that made him eager to sculpt shapes. When Rhina saw his eyes again, every future poem flooded her thoughts, filling them with rhythms and sounds of all the amazing things that were possible. Secretly, she imagined pieces of words as she did when she was a child, the same pieces that would later form the poem emerging from that encounter.

David left Romania to come to North America without knowing what would happen. Dulce María boarded the bus to leave La Vega without knowing either. Sometimes the universe disorders all the pieces, stirring the waters and clouding the riverbeds; it overcasts days and breaks the sluice gates. Then magic dresses up like an everyday miracle and from the furnace of shadows, an invincible love appears.

POEMS BY RHINA ESPAILLAT

Stanzas: I Was Born in the First City...

I was born in the first city
from which this continent rose;
fed by the rivers of all the world
water from my fountain flows.

I grew in tender Quisqueya,
in the valley called Cibao,
shaded by *caimito* trees,
and *papaya*, and *cacao*.

In the garden of my first home,
in my family's loving ways,
I learned to sing and keep customs,
tell old stories and give praise.

The fruit vendor showed her platter,
the candyman hawked his wares;
coffee in the afternoon;
and the Virgin heard our prayers.

Blood of Spain, Haiti, the Gold Coast
courses through my veins: all three—
Taíno, slave and slave-trader—
become one, becoming me,

along with any newcomer—
be he Arab, Chinese, Jew—
for he who sets foot on my land

then becomes my brother too.

Later I learned about exile
enforced when tyrants oppress.
That is why I live so far from
the home I used to possess.

I know time and distance alter
those we meet living afar.
Still, despite all circumstances,
our brothers is what they are.

And, no matter who denies it,
since there's just one earth—no other—
we to whom she's given birth
are children of the one mother.

[*Translated by* Rhina P. Espaillat]

Fourteen Years Old

The maiden moves as if she were
a new sprout that seems too hesitant to bloom.
She looks so young and elusive in her ascent
that she removes herself from the sky, and then
she wakes triggered by the light she now detects.

She moves as if an ardent greenness
climbed all the way up her stem to reach the lace
on her corolla. And her floral face
becomes uneasy over the rebellious airs
and the sound of hosannas everywhere.

Snowing

With thanks to Kurt Semel

It is snowing: the sky has been left bare,
devoid of petals, coins, darts and feathers,
razor blades, hail, syllables cast out,
tears, murky weather.

It is snowing: in the shabby old pine tree
three ravens sleep; behind the windows, the children
watch, surprised by what they see: it's the Wind King
wearing his ermines!

How will the once lush greenery be renewed?
In what shelter will these things be saved,
the gentle, unarmed things, if winter subdues them
and the snow remains?

BIOGRAPHY

RHINA P. ESPAILLAT was born in Santo Domingo in 1932. She spent her childhood in La Vega and has lived in the United States since she was seven years old. At first, she lived in New York where she worked as an English teacher for several years and then Massachusetts where she has been since 1990. She is a poet, short-story writer and essayist in both English and Spanish, and she has published several translations from English to Spanish and vice versa. Rhina Espaillat is a renowned translator. Some of the writers she has translated are Robert Frost, Richard Wilbur, Sor Juana Inés de la Cruz, San Juan de la Cruz, and many more.

Her works have been published in journals, anthologies in English and Spanish, and websites. Rhina Espaillat has won national and international prizes. Among her seventeen collections covering different genres, three are bilingual editions: *The World and the Word / Mundo y palabra; Agua de dos ríos / Water From Two Rivers;* and *El olor de la memoria / The Scent of Memory: Cuentos / Short Stories.*

> The poems *"Coplas: nací en la ciudad primada," "Catorce años"* and *"Nevando"* were unpublished before the publication of *10 dominicanas de Letras. Homenaje & antología* (DWA 2019).

3. **MÉLIDA GARCÍA**

Unwavering Mélida

To MÉLIDA GARCÍA
By Osiris Mosquea

> *I want to leave feeling*
> *my soul return to my childhood*
> *free from the shackles that restrain my wings.*
> Mélida García

Mélida was young when she read her first book, and from that moment on, her passion for reading never left her side. In each book, a new world opened up before her, a universe of entangled adventures spread out on the pages.

She was a girl with unruly hair, thin and chatty, somewhat of a dreamer, but she had a firm temper with a strong sense of humor and irony.

The town she lived in was small and traditional. Everyone knew each other. In the evening after school, instead of playing with the other kids, she would spend long hours at Mr. Carmelo's house; he was a beloved and popular gentleman in town. Mr. Carmelo enjoyed telling her, and anyone interested in listening, the story of how he participated in the Revolution of April 1965, and how he survived the bombing by the gringo troops. Carmelo was an avid reader and his house was full of books; he also read comics and lent books to his visitors so they could take them home.

The cosmos Mélida discovered in books was so vast that she would spend long hours sitting in an old chair on the patio, eagerly reading everything Mr. Carmelo lent her. One of those evenings, after she locked herself up in the fantastic universe of her reading, she suddenly jumped up and said, "I know, I want to be a writer! I will lock my own stories in books." This idea became fixed in her mind.

She spent many days asking herself how to achieve her wish. She did not understand that world and its magnitude.

"I want people to read my work, to know I am a great writer!" She had discovered her vocation and, because she was a child with a sharp imagination, it wasn't long before she wrote her first stories.

Some time later, once she started college, she decided to study education and literature. Both her deep sensibility and political militancy led her way. "For humanity to progress, we must start with education," she declared. And so she did: she dedicated her life to education and writing. Her friends and students admired her literary education, her creativity, and her constant efforts to self-publish her books. She also had an excellent memory, could recite whole paragraphs by heart to her friends and students, complete dialogues from her favorite writers, and could even remember the exact page from where she had extracted them.

Literature was a constant throughout her life, a passion that stayed with her forever; she also loved, loved intensely as those who give themselves completely tend to do. Mélida, with her endless discipline and determination, managed to publish important works and be recognized as the writer she dreamed of becoming.

However, life is unpredictable, and sometimes life wounds us with its sharp thorns. The day the doctors said her life was fading away was a grievous day. She felt as if the news had been delivered in stanzas filled with lies. The revelation kept her on guard and more unwavering than ever. Calm and even humorous, she simply said: "I am not going to die, every day I head out into life and I am reborn."

"Life is only a breath of death and I will not leave until

I write *Mi último deseo / My Last Wish*." And so it was.

The days, swift and determined, sank into the night's shadows, where death thrived inside the body, inside the pulse that made her breath fade away. Until she was found one morning, as always, never split: A whole woman!

STORY BY MÉLIDA GARCÍA

Of What Happened that Terrible Day When Time Decided to Demand Vindications

*For Isidro Pichardo and Nicolás Liranzo,
whom I thought of calling in the middle of the nightmare
that preceded the creation of this story.*

Time was in a bad mood. He was overwhelmed by unpleasant thoughts: I am tired of being blamed for so many misfortunes: that many things perish because too much time has passed over them; that those who have aged in my wake do not want to grow old. That it is necessary to make the best of me, because I am the only thing that does not stop, that is irreversible, and, for that reason, I should be milked as much as possible. That people need me. That many want to have me, but don't; whereas others waste me as if I were worthless and unimportant. That it is because many people are deprived of me that there are so many anomalies in the world: lack of human communication, lack of family affection, late arrivals or non-arrivals to serious commitments, "I just don't have the time."

Then, carrying the burden of his bad mood, time appeared before God and said: "You have to do something so they stop pestering me so much."

God decided to arm himself with patience and listen to time's rosary of complaints.

While the conversation took place, in one of the comfortable rooms of the celestial palace, many things happened in the world beyond God's control: wars started, others ended. Many people were killed and others got married. Some of them from disparate social classes. Beings of all species were conceived and born, new species appeared, new planets were discovered, super sophisticated weapons were created to kill even more people faster than before, and some were so truly sophisticated they could determine their targets on their own. The stars moved closer and their light outshone the Sun. People from other planets decided to help Earth, so they started to relocate people from our "heres" to their "theres," planes and trains changed their routes of circulation and the planes started to run on the rails and the trains flew. With everyone taking advantage of God's distraction, marine and terrestrial animals changed their places of residence and it was wonderful seeing whales, sharks, trout, sea snails, dolphins, crabs, oysters, and lobsters curled up on tree branches, standing on their tails, leaning on clouds, hens, condors, herons, doves, nightingales, ducks... all dancing beneath and above the water. The elderly acquired the youthfulness of children, placing their wrinkles on the faces of children, who looked old, very old. Objects became tired of always being moved by others so they gained mobility. It was marvelous seeing plates, chairs, paintings, pans, pieces of paper, books, buildings, tables, sculptures, pens... walking and running and flying and swimming, and the Sun and the Moon and all the other stars got tired of being still and they started to revolve and Earth appreciated their gesture because she was tired of revolving, and in that moment, she stayed still and musical instruments were used to write. Typewriters, pens, and pencils made music and books hung on walls and paintings were placed on bookshelves and telephones did not transmit sound but rather drawings of messages and vehicles became useless because houses took people from one place to another and love and hate gave each other a hug and made a friendly pact for no aggression, peaceful coexistence, free market, and hate agreed to be less hateful and love agreed to be less loving and this time, hate won again, of course. Then the Devil did something he had been trying to get permission to do for a long time, which God refused to appease: He gathered a group of experts in unimaginable torture techniques so they could create torment harsher than that already available in hell, for the special guests he keeps in his castles of terror (and many more continue to arrive) for whom he requires torment far more infernal.

Many other noteworthy things happened, but I cannot recount them because I do not have enough time.

When God realized all that had gone on, he dourly told time: "You see all the things that happened because you decided to come here and waste my time."

June, 1995

BIOGRAPHY

MÉLIDA GARCÍA REYES was born in Cotuí in 1956. She held a Bachelor of Philosophy and Letters. García Reyes earned a postgraduate degree in Spanish Language and Literature from the Universidad Autónoma de Santo Domingo. She was a part of said distinguished house of studies' Department of Letters' teaching faculty. García Reyes published the following: *Entre nieblas* (stories, 1992); *Brumas* (short novel, 1994); *La floresta* (children's story, 1994); *El innombrable* (poetry, 1995 & 1997); *Desvivencias* (stories, 1997); *Laberinto* (novel, 1998 & 1999); *Oro sulfuro y muerte* (novel, 1999, 2000 & 2001); *Inventario de la noche* (poetry, 2002); *Entre nieblas y otros cuentos* (stories, 2003). Before she passed away in 2005, she published *El último deseo* (stories).

> *"De lo que aconteció el fatídio día en que el tiempo decidió reclamar reivindicaciones"* was originally published in *Entre nieblas y otros cuentos* (Editora Manatí, 2003).

4. **OSIRIS MOSQUEA**

My Color

To OSIRIS MOSQUEA
By José Acosta

The afternoon sun struck down on the road making the asphalt flare as if it were about to burst into flames. It was the beginning of the school year and Osiris, with her backpack over her shoulder, could feel the sun shine on her legs as soon as she left her house. El Colegio Episcopal Jesús el Nazareno was surrounded by tall trees that gave off a cool breeze, not too far from her home. She was keeping her promise to go and get her friend Isabel, so she strayed off the path and turned on La Cruz Street. She was but four houses away from her classmate's home, when she saw a tall man with a disdainful look standing in a doorway. He watched her walk with that elegant, carefree, and cheerful stride common among *quinceañeras*. Then he broke out into jeering laughter.

"Look at this black girl! So ugly! Kinky hair!" He yelled. "If she were white she wouldn't touch the ground."

Osiris was startled by the sudden onslaught. She picked up her pace and looked back every now and then to make sure the man was not following her. She made it to Isabel's house and nervously knocked on the door.

Her friend opened up.

"What's wrong?" She asked. "You look like you saw a ghost."

"It's nothing." Osiris replied, calmer now. "A pervert shouted some nasty things at me."

As they walked to school, Osiris told her friend all the details of what happened.

The next day, the man's hands rested on the doorframe as he doubled his volley of insults. Osiris noticed he was screaming at her from a barbershop. The establishment was oval-shaped and looked dark inside from the sidewalk. One could hardly make out the barber's heavy chair and a long wooden bench.

"I have never seen such an ugly and uppity black girl." The man screamed at her. "Didn't you know that black people are pig food? Didn't you, you kinky hair!"

By the fourth day of being subjected to the barber's taunts, Osiris understood that he was not going to stop. Harassing her had become a part of his daily routine, to the point of even leaving one of his customers unattended to run to the door and badmouth her. Deep down, the barber's attitude was more surprising to her than it was upsetting. She asked herself, "Why does he do that?" but she didn't dare ask him. The barber confused her surprise for indifference. It was this perceived indifference that encouraged him to harass her.

"One day you will realize you're black," he yelled on one occasion. "And then I'll see you walk with your head down, kinky hair!"

Osiris had a wall that protected her from the world's evils: An education she acquired by reading. Her father instilled that love for reading in her. After reading the daily newspaper, he would hand her the culture and general interest sections. Reading provided her with the tools that turned her over time, into an important writer and a sensitive and self-sacrificing teacher. From a very early age, and as a result of her being an avid reader, she formed a very clear and firm idea of who she was as a person and of the goals she wanted to achieve in life. The barber's words, no matter how hurtful and spiteful they were, simply clashed against a personality like Osiris' without leaving a trace behind.

One afternoon, while the barber launched a string of insults at her, Osiris, full of courage, faced her attacker and requested permission to come inside the barbershop. The man, clearly surprised, stepped aside and invited her in. The girl's eyes drifted across the walls until she found what she was looking for.

"I was wrong," she said. "I could have sworn there were no mirrors in here."

"Why wouldn't there be any mirrors in a barbershop!" He exclaimed. "Besides black, you're stupid?"

"Then you must be blind," Osiris replied. "Because if you weren't blind you'd realize by looking in the mirror that, if I'm black, so are you, and I bet that before going bald, your hair was just as curly as mine."

The barber stood in front of the mirror, stared at himself for a longtime and looked down. From that day on, every time Osiris walked by the barbershop, the man smiled and yelled:

"My color! That's how I like black girls, proud of their race! The world can fall apart and no one will keep this black girl from being successful in her life!"

And so it was.

POEMS BY OSIRIS MOSQUEA

In the Almost Island

You love this city of no one, of escapes…
you navigate the almost island
where a lady in the middle of the Hudson
with airs of a queen—French, by the way—
greets you, welcomes you and seduces you
by gifting you with fear in advance
freedom conditioned by some words in parenthesis
in which everything, everything is perfect day after day

You swing from this pendulum of dreams
traveling in the vast trunk of the train
with the exact dosage to ignore everything
living hours of a minute and a half
snatching from luck
Roosevelt's green and enigmatic smile
in a constellation of egos to not lose it all

In this city that I too live in
the centaur on Wall Street
puts on the miter and the bicorn
blesses the coins that quenched by poison
travel the streets of Manhattan
where the shipwrecks are not spoken of
nor are the times that discreet nostalgia
hangs on the wings of birds
that blindly commit suicide
against the Broadway lights' muzzles

You live in this city for all

of walls vomiting last names like yours, like mine
empty and distant names
of those deceased in others' brawls
spied upon by the eyes of the buildings
traveling fastened to the fear-belt
that swallows us into a mass grave
sweating the same blood that clings to the razor blade.

Immigrating Towards Whitman

> *The train is a piece of the city that fades away.*
> Vicente Huidobro

A moon of hope
wanes in every face.

A sleepy yawn
curdled with sadness
permeates the yearning.

An urgent coffee settles with sleep
it's filtered by veins
like a silent metaphor
awake.

To my right
a psalm
joyful and painful
So what!

The trains snore
and from their wombs a visceral cry rises
millions of last names and accents
immigrating toward Whitman

refusing oblivion.

At every station
a volley of music
deflowers thoughts.

A sad *bandoneón*

carries one of Gardel's tangos in the air
a lazy guitar
accompanies the nostalgia
of a Mexican *corrido*
and neither the Andean flute
nor a restless *bachata* matter
when a rap song strikes my ears,
meanwhile, some lustful eyes undress me.

The drumbeats add a different tone
black-African blood
white-Caribbean-American
proclaim a broken
cry, a desert
rather than another shore.

I tear a Rulfo story apart
I become undone by speculations
by memories perhaps
and surprisingly submissive
I wait for the train.

God, Where Were You When the Angel Lost its Wings?

> For Ali Ismail, the Iraqi boy that lost his arms during the first bombings of the north American invasion of Iraq (2003).
>
> *There are blows in life, so powerful...*
> Cesar Vallejo

Run Ali
run
ask Scheherazade
for an eternal story
to deceive death.

Run
the forty thieves have arrived
and there is no time
for psalms at noon.

You see
God is deaf
blind are the angels
that hide with a finger
the ghost that kills you.

On the gods' altars
the ashes of the dead.

A heart weeps in the mosque
and you are mutilated in the cybernetic desert
of the computer
on the television that spits on your face
to gain followers.

And you, Ali
remain on the bed
amid a flutter of mutilated wings
where an alphabet of sheets rescues you.

A knot trembles in my throat
from the weight of your eyes
I want to weave you a promise
with the transparent thread of your tears
when you descend from death
to the shore of the Euphrates
where never
ever,
even if God hears you,
you
will never be the same.

BIOGRAPHY

OSIRIS MOSQUEA was born in San Francisco de Macorís, Dominican Republic. She attended the Universidad Autónoma de Santo Domingo (U.A.S.D.) where she earned a Bachelor of Arts in accounting. She holds a Master of Arts in Spanish Language and Literature from the City College of New York. Mosquea is a poet and narrator. She is a founding member of *Trazarte Huellas Creativas* in New York City and coeditor of *Revista Trazos*. Her work has been published in magazines, newspapers and anthologies in the United States and other parts of the world: *Antología Poética Terre de Poétes Terre de Paix* (Paris, 2007); *Un poema a Pablo Neruda*, Isla Negra (Santiago de Chile, 2010); *Antología del XIV Encuentro Internacional de Poetas en Zamora* (Michoacan, 2010); *Noches de vino y rosas. La antología* (New York, 2010); *Mujeres de palabra. Poética y antología* (New York, 2010); *Nostalgias de arena* (Santo Domingo, 2011). Her poetry publications include: *Una mujer: Todas las mujeres* (miCielo ediciones, Mexico, 2015); *Viandante en Nueva York* (Artepoética Press, New York, 2013); and *Raga del tiempo* (Santo Domingo, 2009). As a narrator, she published *De segunda mano* (Books & Smith, New York, 2018).

The poem *"En la suerte de la isla"* was included in *Viandante en Nueva York* (Artepoética Press, 2013) and both *"Inmigrando hacia Whitman"* and *"Dónde estabas Dios cuando el ángel perdió sus alas"* appear in *Raga del tiempo* (Editorial Argos, 2009).

5. JOSEFINA BÁEZ

Matches

To JOSEFINA BÁEZ
By Keiselim A. Montás

She started speaking Pig Latin as soon as she started speaking in complete sentences: "olyhay owcay!" She would not stay quiet, nor stay put; she rushed through everything, lively and curious as she was. They say she could see light in the darkest places, which was why she was the best at hide-and-seek. She could find the other players right away and because she could not hide her luminance, they would find her right away too. Trina, the midwife who brought her and her nine siblings into the world fondly named her "Matches." For that same reason, everyone in the neighborhood (from the adults to the ones her own age) used to say that when she grew up she was going to work for the Electric Company, considering there were power outages all the time.

Perhaps because she was the youngest of ten kids, she knew—in body and soul—that she was taken care of, safe and protected; spoiled the way working class girls are. Due to that freedom, she always aspired to the game, to play: tag, the handkerchief, hide-and-seek, volleyball, Parcheesi, the little house, cooking, to plant, and shower under the pouring rain. She says that when she was a year old she lost the Durango, Luis Báez, her dad; but instead of absence, there was a "magical presence. A powerful and whole presence." That is where Luz María Pérez, Báez's widow, sheds light on the axis of every aspect of her life and the center from where all spirals revolve; the lady who "responsibly took care of things, as it was her right," and who she says she wants to be like. They had to call her Luz!

As if it were a spiral, playing (Da' Play) started to become a constant in life: The constant in life, the constancy, the constant:

Playing is and will be the constant. The spiral revolved around the world of the house. At age five, back when the streets of Santa Rosa and 24 de Abril set the limits of that world, she believed it was "biiiiiiiiiiiig." As the girl grew, the limits grew with her: all the way to her grandmother's house, where every mango was named after a grandchild, to the park where the orange sellers could be found, to the Papagayo Theater and the lollipop sellers nearby, to the cockfights' cockpit, to the town limits and the airfield. By age twelve, the world expanded to New York, and the spiral shrunk towards the center of 107th Street, extending to 109th, to 125th, to Brandeis High School on 84th, to 14th, and to Delancy Street.

Two things marked her upon her arrival in November of 1972: Noticing how, upon breathing, it looked like one was smoking or "smoking without smoking." For her, this and learning how they jumped rope made New York, New York. That quick, two-roped game of Double Dutch was a revelation. It was as if the double-rope's rhythmical skip were an echo to that spiral. The acquisition of a new language (from that very English of her own, the one she began to speak by three, to this American English that required her to twist her mouth like that to say things), along with the music she started to absorb, forged in her a here and there consciousness: Billie Holiday and Cuco Valoy. This is how she realized she really liked being in places where she didn't speak the language because it gave her more freedom and space to learn and be alert.

Just like that, she traveled from La Romana to New York, from Washington Heights to India. Yes, she makes it to India, and sees that there are also lots of mangos there. There are also plantains, lots of plantains (thin ones, thick ones, some with red skin), and a lot of dark-skinned people that weren't aware of their darkness either. That too made her closer to India, as its *dulce de leche* did. With her Guru (of Being), she started to turn life's mirror in her own direction. She took dance classes, studied philosophy and became interested in the practice of silence, in silence; the silence "like a shore to access your essence." Over thirty years in a relationship with India and she knows that there—just like every place in the world—you encounter the same issues.

It is life's constancy, that spiral, and the search for light since she was little that gave us Josefina Báez, Dominican-York, ArteSana, storyteller, performer, writer, theater director, devotee and alchemist of the creative life process. Josefina, who I saw from my car as I drove north on the Harlem River Drive on a sunny day, walked along the riverside dressed in white, scarf in the air (in essence); she told me she was seeking the light. I told her that in that sense, she was like her mother, Luz, who by giving birth to her gave us "all possible light, all necessary light" for those of us who have been in her presence know ourselves to be illuminated, even when she continues to seek for the light.

Postscript: I have weaved these words on paper, but the words (*the Words*) and the inner light have always belonged to Josefina Baéz.

NARRATIVE TEXTS BY JOSEFINA BÁEZ

Micro-story 1

Yes. No. Was always the answer.
And then we started to weave the questions.

Micro-story 2

If not. Always. The answer.
And then we started to weave.
Questions.

Ana and Anand

Ana and Anand are seven years old.
Ana and Anand are interpreters
and translators.

In the waiting room of the Department of Transportation in Harlem.
There are a lot of people today.
Different languages are heard.
And we are all of color.
A variety of colors... 'like the birds that come from faraway.'

Divided and separated by two empty chairs are the two
families of the story.
Of the story. With their stories.
Each family has a father, a mother.
A boy in the family on the right.
And a girl in the family on the left.
The girl on the left is independent, she knows what it is to look
and smile at the same time, she invites the boy on the right.
The two of them begin to run, thinking with the heart. About the
heart.
The two move with a revolution three times the energy
of their years multiplied by the possible joy that urges them
to paint the somber room with light.
The fathers from each family said at the same time and without
looking
at each other:
Meena, María.
But the mothers, Meena and María, looked at each other and
smiled.
They agreed with their little ones' actions. And
they sealed their deal with a shrug.

The men shoook their heads. Each of them in their own particular way.
One with a no that looked like a yes.
The other with a no that he repeated so many times it became a nonononononono.
I could almost hear them say:

"You don't discipline him. That little girl we don't even know. She is not like us. That is why she is like that. Children are raised differently here. If it were my country…"

"You don't discipline her. We don't know that little boy. He is not like us. That is why he is like that. Growing up on his own. Children are raised differently here. If this were my country…"

Ana and Anand pretended they were planes.
Their bodies formed crosses, they flapped their wings, took off, landed;
standing straight as they moved forward; their wings-arms-wings dropped to turn right.
There is turbulence.
Again, standing straight. Heading forwards. The plane shrinks and becomes each of their hands. They continue their routes in their multiverses, followed closely by their mothers' gazes.
Every time they looked up at a part of the sky where their planes traveled,
the little ones called out the colors that only they could see.
Rojo. Yerra. Amarillo. Pasupu.
Verde. Peccha. Azul. Neeli.
Sunsets and dawns. Days of rain. Monsoon. Days of sun.
As remote as Harlem to that distant place we are all supposed to know where it is.

Rojo. Yerra. Amarillo. Pasupu.
Verde. Peccha. Azul. Neeli.
The passports pose, repose and rest on the
mothers' laps, they were trying to skip the long lines and

countless payments made in the countries of origin; official
permit to be an "NRI" and an "Absent Dominican;" taking
the final step towards the frenzy of the dream often spoken about
around here, without screaming; quietly appreciating the begging
prayers and the lamps made in return for just a dream.
For just a dream. Just one.
One.
Calmly, the passports, identified the countries, like the
bronze medal athlete who retraces all his steps from all the
times-yesterday, today and tomorrow.
Passport of the Republic of India.
Passport of the Dominican Republic.

Anand's parents were from Hyderabad.
Ana's parents were from Higüey.

Meena, with her superstition twisted into braids. And María with
hers uncurled, both entertained themselves by singing and
complaining. Recounting the benefits lost and gained during
this first year in New York.
A New York in which they did the same things they did in their
countries.
A New York that does not appear on postcards.
A New York where they were yet to see the first blonde *gringo*
who they had seen so many times in their countries.

Meena and María were the sorcerers of the sweets made of milk.
Over there in Hyderabad.
Over there in Higüey.
The magic, alchemy mixed with family secrets. Open
secrets. Tricks that everyone knows. The recipes of a whole town.
That are now on the web.
Cardamomo. Dad. Silver paper. Cashews from La Enea.

María brought Higüey on her earrings with the Virgen and the
    Basílica.
Meena brought Hyderabad on her pearl earrings bought

in Basheer Bagh.

Rojo. Amarillo. Verde. Azul. Amarillo. Pasupu. Yerra. Neeli. Peccha.

Anand spoke in Telugu
And Ana replied in Spanish.
Ana spoke to him in Spanish
And Anand replied in Telugu.

Rojo. Yerra. Amarillo. Pasupu. Verde. Peccha. Azul. Neeli.
The planes-pilots-pilots-planes created and painted colors
in two languages as they traveled until their parents
were called upon, here on 125th.
They smiled as they said goodbye. And within the first three steps
        closer to their parents, their little bodies assumed the
posture of the interpreter.

"Who filled this application?"
"Me."
"Where is this little voice coming from?"
They replied simultaneously from the other side of the two windows where a clerk assisted our families.
"This voice is coming from my mouth."
Replied the owners of colors, in languages spoken at home, and names with the letter A in their initials.

They chewed on their answers with smiles, while the parents carried them.
In that moment, Anand said the colors in Spanish.
Ana in Telugu.

BIOGRAPHY

JOSEFINA BÁEZ [La Romana, Dominican Republic / United States]. ArteSana, storyteller and performer. Founder and director of Ay Ombe Theatre (since April 1986). Alchemist of the process of creative life and creator of Performance Autology, a creative process based on the autobiography and well being of the doer. Books published: *Dominicanish, Comrade, Bliss Ain't Playing* (translated into Russian, Spanish, Swedish, Italian, Hindi and Portuguese), *Dramaturgia I & II, Como la una/Como Uma. Latin In* (anthology of autology) and *¿Por qué mi nombre es Marysol?* (a story for girls and boys). www.josefinabaez.com.

"*Microcuento 1*" and "*Microcuento 2*" were published in *As Is E'. Textos reunidos de Josefina Báez* (I Om Be Press, 2015). "*Ana y Anand*" was published in *Vislumbres. India & Iberoamérica Vol. 1* (Embassy of Spain in India 2008).

6.   AURORA ARIAS

True History of a Tropical Night

To AURORA ARIAS
By Néstor E. Rodríguez

Aurora Arias could have been born in Cyprus, Saint Martin, New Guinea, or any of the other divided islands found in the world. However, providence wanted her to be born in the Dominican Republic, and to have friends in four categories: "ordinary, good, very bad and sad," as a poem by a friend of mine conveys. I, her melancholic biographer, belong to the sad group. Perhaps that is why she has been telling me things with a nearly ritualistic regularity for some years now. For instance, during one of our endless conversations, I found out that she was born on the twenty-second of March on the verge of midnight, when the Sun left Pisces and moved into Aries. Her personality, therefore, oscillates between the marvel that guides all of those born under the last of the zodiac signs and the distinctive stubbornness of those born under the first of the signs: the Arians that announce the beginnings and despise endings. It is possible that the liminal condition of the eventuality of her birth is at the core of her nature as a mediator, her reticence towards any sign of falseness, and her faith in good-willed people. So many traces of utopianism could not indicate any other path but that of fabulation. Aurora becoming a writer was clearly a matter of destiny because, as we know, when something is meant for you, resisting is useless. My heroine writes the way she lives, with the same involuntary perseverance of her respiration and oblivious to all falsehood. To do so, she digests the quotidian by parts, like ruminants. Everything that lives becomes literature. Some years ago we met at that little piece of sea called Bayahibe, "place of water," in Taíno. We walked passed the dividing line between the Dominicans' beach to access the foreigners Arcadia. Immediately after, two compatriots dressed like colonists from the British Empire in

Africa positioned themselves just a couple of meters away from us. Not too far away, where the finest sand in the world shone, hundreds of European bodies enjoyed the soft evening light. They wandered topless on the shore, stretched their legs on lustrous beach chairs, ordered martinis from Viernes and braids from the kind natives. Between them, our copper-colored continents stood out like two enemy pennants amid a battle. The tragicomic scene lasted the ten minutes we were there, but its burden followed us into the early morning. By then, we were far away from the hotel and its shiny little bracelets, having a bitter conversation that months later became one of Aurora's perfect tales. It is due to stories of this depth and skill that, if someone asked me what contemporary Dominican literature would pass the test of time, I would undoubtedly start the list with Aurora's ineffable narrative; Aurora, born on the twenty-second of March, on the verge of midnight, when the Sun left Pisces and moved into Aries.

SHORT STORY BY AURORA ARIAS

Driving Around

Masters in the art of driving around, Olivia and Fito roll down the City's avenues.

Olivia, 23, a recent graduate with a degree in economics, unemployed, has an it's-all-cool kind of face.

Fito, 27, son of a former leftist veteran, tries to sell insurance policies.

For some time now they like going out to have fun with Carmina. They turn in any direction and there she is, at some corner, waiting for them. Luckily, she is always on foot. She shows up happy and smelling like perfume. They take off.

On the way, Olivia, who has the habit of thinking out loud says:
"The city is so cool at nighttime, isn't it? To think that for some people, the city isn't even that cool. To think that more than—I don't remember the exact number—of the population lives in complete poverty. To think that if no one went out of their way to visit the poor neighborhoods, no one would notice anything, how about that?"

Then, Carmina, sitting in the backseat says:
"Poverty is a karmic issue that neither politicians, nor sociologists or economists will ever be able to solve."

(That's the bad thing about Carmina. She is quick to play her esoteric cards! Fito reflects.) He replies:
"That's not true, if anything is going to change in this country, it

depends on the youth!"

At the traffic light before Güibia, one of the many karmic indigent people, according to Carmina, whose present, past, and future depend on the youth, according to Fito, rushes his sponge full of soap and dirty water onto the windshield of Fito and Olivia's car, the same car they bought with help from their parents.

Olivia continues to reflect:
"Who is more indigent: You and I, middle class, but still depending on our parents or that indigent man that lives off what people give him for cleaning their windshields? We don't own our own houses either! We just got married, right, Fito? And we still can't save any money to buy ourselves an apartment..."

To drive by Güibia as the rain pours is part of the Maná song playing on the radio to the beat of Fito's voice, he is scolding the indigent man for getting his windshield dirty with the sponge. Now the windshield is covered with dirty water, salt residue, and detergent. It's only when it rains like this that the streets flood and the sea looks so happy. Sometimes, while one side of the city is hot and sweating to death, a downpour suddenly refreshes the other side.

"The local authorities refuse to do anything to solve the flooding problem," Fito says sitting behind the wheel, trying to dive through the road.
"That's what I'm saying, Fito, that what we experience in this country is a karmic issue," Carmina replies. "We elect our own governors. You know, cause and effect."

(Here we go again!)

"Fito, do you remember when we went to Havana on our honeymoon and we met Emilio?" —Olivia's young and bright eyes were fixed on the lights coming in from outside. Then, turning towards Carmina, she carries on— "Emilio was the coolest guy! He worked at a hotel in Varadero where he taught tourists how to windsurf."

"And what happened to him?" Carmina asks.
"Nothing, just one day he went into the sea on his windsurf and he slowly disappeared into the horizon. They say he surfed all the way to Florida, pretty cool, huh?"

They turn down one of the seafront's deadly curves, leaving the obelisk behind them. Fito silently remembers brave Emilio again.
"And what is this Emilio's sign?" Carmina asks.

(What is truly stupid and surprising is that someone is capable of categorizing others based on their signs, horoscopes and all that shit! What I can't take is this obsession with predicting, with killing whatever life has left of unexplored chance! Fito thinks.)

From the backseat, Carmina examines Fito's cranial chakras, which are blocked by anger and disappointment. That's the good thing about Carmina, she understands everyone. That is why she ends up becoming so addictive, even when some people believe otherwise. That is why they had gotten used to driving around with her everywhere. That's why they picked her up all the time!

They drive by the old, now abandoned building where the Capri ice cream shop used to be. The rain clears up. The traffic light is red.

"Once," Carmina says, changing the subject, "my grandmother won the lottery and took me and my sisters out to eat ice cream. It was the first time we went out for ice cream in our lives. And we went to Capri! We were so happy that when the waiter arrived with the order, we couldn't control our excitement and we accidently knocked the tray from his hands. We made a huge mess; we threw ourselves on the floor, eager for strawberry ice cream with cookies and whipped cream with a cherry on top. My grandmother was so completely freaked out, she never took us anywhere again."

Olivia can't stop laughing. Her laughter takes a different course as they turn toward 19 de Marzo Street.

"Fito, stop at that corner store." Olivia demands.

He is always the one that has to get out of the car to please Olivia, and, while he is at it, to please himself. Fito is a promoter of legal drugs. Aaahh! Life can be appreciated from a fresher perspective with a beer in hand. Also, if the youth were the future, what would become of the future without days like these, driving around and having a beer every now and then? Will their inevitable destiny be to visit, like their parents, the temples of an eternal incomprehension?

Starting at Las Damas, the memories emerge: driving around Constanza with Carmina; driving around Samaná with Carmina; Carmina and them in Bayahibe, driving around in a boat headed to Saona; the nights in Santiago, driving around with Carmina...

"All things considered, ladies and gentlemen, either way, this country really is cool. We really do joke around and have a good time, don't we?" Olivia says out loud as they approach Meriño.

BIOGRAPHY

AURORA ARIAS. Dominican poet and narrator. Arias has published two books of poetry, *Vivienda de pájaro* and *Piano lila*. She has published three books of stories, *Invi Paradise, Fin de mundo*, and *Emoticons*. Her poems and stories have been translated into English, French, German, Icelandic, Bengali, and Italian, and have been selected by different anthologies such as *Common Threads: Afro Hispanic Women's Literature* (USA, 1998), *Sólo cuento* (México, 2010), *Les bonnes nouvelles de l'Amérique latine* (Francia, 2011), *Un lugar en la memoria: Relatos de dictaduras en América Latina* (Argentina, 2016), *Indómita y brava: Antología de poetas dominicanos contemporáneos* (Spain, 2017), and *No creo que yo esté aquí de más, Antología poética* (Spain, 2018).

Currently, she lives in the United States where she carries out workshops and other literary activities.

"Dando ruedas" was included in *Fin de mundo y otros relatos* (Editorial Universidad de Puerto Rico, 2000).

7. **YRENE SANTOS**

Yrene Santos López

To YRENE SANTOS
By Carlos Aguasaco

They say in Villa Tapia that when María Yrene came to this world the whole town remained silent. That Thursday morning in June, the midwife arrived at the house of the López family where their daughter, Polonia, was about to give birth. When José Santos rushed over the night before to notify her that his wife was about to have the baby, she calmly replied while chewing on *mangú*, "Don't worry, José, that baby girl is going to be born at dawn. Go home and wait." José ran home to tell Polonia that the baby would be born the next morning. Yes it would be a girl, the midwife was never wrong. For years she had been foretelling the biological gender of all the babies in town with a scientific accuracy. Some even suspected she had X-Ray vision because on one occasion, she warned a policeman of a malignant tumor that had started to invade his lungs. María Yrene was born before Cibaeño—that's what the López family called their rooster—crowed two times. The wide-armed woman lifted her up in the air, turned her twice to inspect all of the parts of her body, and to count her fingers. After a while, amid the expectation of all those present, she declared the baby had been born healthy and whole. Polonia looked at her daughter from the bed and asked to be given the baby to bless her and kiss her forehead.

The Santos López settled in a mildly desolate alley where they built a wooden house. Nowadays, that place is known as *"El Callejón de los Poetas"* (The Poets Alley), and writers from all over the world go there to visit the girl, now a woman, a professor, writer, mother, immigrant, and poet. They say that one day, Tomás Galán went all the way there in a new SUV and left the next morning on a mototaxi.

María Yrene and her family cultivated the plot and gathered coffee. Life, although humble, was happy in that corner of the world. At the age of nine, María Yrene saw the sea for the first time. Her impression was that of being in front of a huge plate of spinach soup that she wanted to devour by diving in for a swim.

At school, her teacher, Alfredo Soriano taught her to read and write. María Yrene was not a good student, that's the truth, but she has always been a good actress. One day, Professor Freddy (that's what they called Alfredo) caught her pretending to be the teacher. Her impersonation was so graceful and detail-oriented that he silently waited for her to finish her imaginary lesson. Then he said, "Let's see, María Yrene," and took her to a corner of the classroom. "From now on, I play the teacher part and you play the role of the diligent student." The girl agreed under the condition that soon, she would be allowed to play the part of the teacher. "It's just that I like to write in red pencil," she said with a smile.

When María Yrene turned fifteen, she did not celebrate by wearing an expensive dress, nor did she have a party. Rather, she celebrated with a book of poems where she read César Vallejo for the first time with a side of cake. It was a bittersweet day because she realized that she had found her path, but she also understood she would have to leave Villa Tapia. By sixteen, she relocated to the capital to go to the Universidad Autónoma. There, she participated in theater groups and literary workshops. She met Zaida Corniel, Marianela Medrano, Aurora Arias, Ángela Hernández, and Emelda Ramos. During that time, her writing grew under Mateo Morrison's mentorship. From there, she joined the Generation of '80.

Once she finished college, María Yrene got married to a man whose name I cannot recall, despite how hard I try. After she became a mother, she immigrated with her family to New York and became a high school teacher. She educated Óliver, Álex, and Pilar on her own here as well. Professor Daisy Cocco de Filippis invited her to participate in her literary circle, which is how she started to occupy a visible place in the literary scene of her new city. It was at Bread and Roses Integrated Arts High School that I, Carlos Aguasaco, stepped onto the stage of her life. We met in the year two thousand as Spanish teachers and since then, we have grown as writers and friends. Together, we lived through 9/11, her separation, my children's birth, her parent's death, William Beltran's departure, trips to festivals in Mexico, Colombia, Cuba, the Dominican Republic, Puerto Rico, Honduras and Spain. Through the years, her first name, "María," was left behind, as she became known in the literary world as Yrene Santos. I am privileged to have all of her books of poetry, *Desnudez del silencio* (1988), *Reencuentro* (1997), *El incansable juego* (2002), *Después de la lluvia* (2009), *Me sorprendió geométrica* (2013), *Por el asombro* (2015), and *Septiembre casi termina* (2016). Along with Carlos Velásquez Torres, we organized The Americas Poetry Festival of New York (poetryny.com).

To come full circle, I will reveal one of the secrets of our friendship by explaining the beginning of this story. Since we met, Yrene and I take advantage of every space of shared solitude on planes, in waiting areas at airports, on the subway and in offices, to talk about poetry. Indeed, for years we have been discussing the origin of metaphors, their logic, and their variations through time. Together we have read Lakoff and Emerson out loud. On one occasion I told her each word, quoting Emerson, "is fossil poetry." She disagreed, replying, "Carlitos—let me be clear—nothing is more alive than language." To return to the place where this all started, in Villa Tapia they say that when María Yrene Santos López came to this world, the whole town remained silent. Since then, like that day in 1963, every time Yrene reads her poems, those of us that surround her await her diaphanous smile and the music of her voice turned into poetry.

POEMS BY YRENE SANTOS

The Woman

Today I saw a woman whose bones wept
in them memories dwell
they weave her sleep as ruined as her feet
her hands, her trails of flesh
meanwhile, head down, her eyes closed slide to the earth
her half-naked back ponders rumors of the lived years
the memories are lost with hunger
hunger catapults any sign of joy.
Today I saw a woman wrapped in a pinkish hue
all the way down to where her two paths begin
with her tired head and her hair an inch long
she is touching her broad belly and knees
as she stands on any step at a train station.
At this time, fewer feet drag the fatigue of a long
day
and less fingers grasp on the tenderness that instants before
brushed arms, thighs, bellies or were geometrized
on a warm sofa, a hot bed or a cool floor.
And today I brought that woman in my purse
to keep her alive dignified whole,
in a room with my bookshelves.

Certainty

When I leave, the size of the house
they carry me in will not matter,
there will not be enough room for all my baggage,
so there is no need to worry,
if the house is made of wood, metal, has glass windows or,
simply has no windows at all.
Honestly, what I want to make sure
is that poetry and music
are the impeccable and loyal decoration
of the ceiling and all its walls.

3

A wound unfolds in the sky when hearts on earth
blink incessantly from waiting.

4

How I would like to roam inside you
to search for the origin of that river that runs through your moons
when the night is near
and it changes the course of your laughter.

BIOGRAPHY

YRENE SANTOS (Villa Tapia, Hermanas Mirabal Province, Dominican Republic, 1963) is a writer and professor at the City University of New York (CUNY) and St. John's University.

Published books: *Septiembre casi termina* (Dominican Republic, 2016), *Por el asombro* (Ecuador, 2015), *Me sorprendió geométrica* (New York, 2013), *Después de la lluvia* (Dominican Republic, 2009), *Por si alguien llega* (New York, 2009), *El incansable juego* (Dominican Republic, 2002), *Reencuentro* (New York, 1997), *Desnudez del silencio* (Dominican Republic, 1988). Co-author of the book: *Desde la diáspora: cuentos y poemas de niños y niñas dominicanas* (New York, 2005).

As a poet, two festivals have been dedicated to her: the X Feria de Escritores Dominicanos, organized by the Dominican Commissioner of Culture in New York (2016), and the 10 Feria Internacional del Libro de Escritoras Dominicanas, organized by the Center for the Development of the Dominican Woman (DWDC), also in New York (2013). She has participated in conferences, book fairs, and international poetry festivals. In 2012, Pregones Theater interpreted her work under the direction of Puerto Rican actress and director, Míriam Colón. She co-organizes The Americas Poetry Festival of New York (poetryny.com) with Carlos Aguasaco. Her works have been translated into English, French and Italian.

The poems "La mujer," "3," and "4" appear in *Septiembre casi termina* (Editora Nacional, 2016), and "Certeza" in *Versos Estivales. Antología Poética* (Books & Smith, 2018).

8.   MARIANELA MEDRANO

Marianela Medrano: Sensibility and Resilience

To MARIANELA MEDRANO
By Aurora Arias

My father walks slow memory of ink
he looks at us surprised (at my memory and me).
I am five years old
I am hurt by the slamming door that engulfs us.
I learn to write my name.
Marianela Medrano

The first time I saw her I thought she was too serious for a girl in her early twenties. Her beautiful curly hair seemed to smile for her. It must have been towards the end of February 1987, on a bright and busy evening; like any other evening in Santo Domingo. We were sitting in front of Mateo Morrison's big-boy figure, in the small office where he directed the cultural supplement, *Aquí,* for the evening newspaper, *La Noticia*. We were in the company of Yrene Santos, Ylonka Nacidit Perdomo, Nelly Ciprián, and Mayra Gutiérrez.

We were, unknowingly, the 6 women poets that emerged in the spring of '87 from the drawers of invisibility to the Dominican literary world; a world dominated almost exclusively by men. The National Library organized a recital with the pomp and ardent support of Chiqui Vicioso, who was already an established poet; Juan Bosch, Mrs. Carmen Quidiello, and Morrison were in attendance. This poetic recital inaugurated a series of readings at cultural centers, libraries, universities, parks, streets, city halls, and, on one unforgettable occasion, amid a nightclub's dim lights in Barahona, San Pedro de Macorís, Santiago, Bonao, La Vega, Salcedo, and other towns of the interior.

During that first meeting, Marianela said she was a native of Copey, a county of Montecristi, northeast of the country. She said that she came from a large family living in Bonao. From there the young poet moved to Santo Domingo to work for a real estate agency as a receptionist while she continued writing poems between phone calls. The publication of Oficio de vivir, her first poetry collection, brought her to Mateo and the rest of us. Apart from *Oficio de vivir*, Marianela had an early start as a member of the *Núcleo Literario La Peguera* in Bonao; she was the only woman among the members.

Months later, Marianela published *Los alegres ojos de la tristeza*, her second volume of poetry. Between coordinating meetings with Mateo, walks down El Conde, poetry readings, literary gatherings at Chiqui's house, endless conversations, and laughter, our friendship grew stronger. I discovered that behind what at first seemed to me an excess of seriousness, there was an acute sensitivity in which poetry was the main weapon.

Leaving the Village

Perhaps it was this combination of poetic and spiritual sensitivity and resilience, which led the young female poet from Copey and Bonao to seek independence from her father's house in the late eighties, working an office shift in the capital to support herself so she wouldn't have to give up writing, to later to immigrate to the United States.

"Anyone who has left their village to test their luck elsewhere knows that it is the moment you leave when the real endeavor to gain personal strength, to search for an identity begins," the poet would reflect years later in her essay "*La diáspora como experiencia cultural.*"

When she decided to leave the village, Marianela was familiar with what she called "exile's spinning nightmare" from her father's experience. He had emigrated from the island to the United States, and he experienced Nixon's and Gerald Ford's America. Marianela's first encounter would be George Bush Senior. Even though they were from different decades and time periods, both father and daughter shared the same goal: to get away from a Dominican Republic governed by Joaquín Balaguer ever since the years of the dictator Rafael Leonidas Trujillo.

In 1990, Marianela settled in Connecticut with her son, Noé, the one that "was born in Harlem" (poem "Post-Generation X"), who is currently an up and coming visual artist living in Westville, New Haven, CT. The poet from Copey learned English and started to clear the way for her own path in that vast, diverse, competitive territory that was at once the familiar and foreign territory of the diaspora/s in the United States. Her poetry quickly connected with other poetic voices from the New York and Connecticut area—all the way from the literary gatherings at La Casa Cultural Julia de Burgos, in the classrooms of Yale in New Haven, to the Tertulia de Escritoras Dominicanas that met in Daisy Cocco Filippis living room in Queens, NY.

By the beginning of the new millennium, Marianela had published two more collections of poetry: *Regando esencias / The Scent of Waiting*, her first bilingual book, and *Curada de espantos*, published by Torremozas in Spain. She obtained a BA in Sciences from SUNY State College, an MA in Counseling from Western Connecticut State University, and had previously been certified as a poetry therapist by the National Federation for Poetry Therapy.

Is poetry like a blank page through which the strongest emotional pain, the slightest or most intense joy, fear, solitude, the deepest cry can find a means of expression? Does it have a tangible utility; art in the service of psychology? Some resist this idea. I have seen Marianela more than once—equipped with all the sensibility and resilience that characterizes her—defend the use of poetry as a tool for emotional healing at panels and in literary conversations. Her sensitivity and resilience had found a fascinating outlet in poetry therapy.

For some time, the poet and therapist managed the mental health and recreational services at an intergenerational community in Danbury, CT, where 150 elderly and 37 families lived side by side. Later on, she directed the Counseling Center at Naugatuck Valley Community College, exploring poetry therapy and organizing her own workshops, which combined psychology with the arts, especially writing. Poetry by Rumi, Mirabai, Octavio Paz, Julia de Burgos, Ntozake Shange, Aída Cartagena, Adrienne Rich, and so many other poets made an impression on her, in the same way practicing meditation, yoga and Buddhism had. She later strengthened her interest in these things, earning a doctorate in transpersonal psychology and her approach to Buddhist and Christian monasteries in the United States and India.

By the end of the nineties, Medrano's poetry had been published by the Brooklyn Review, Sisters of Caliban, Callaloo, and Surgai, among other literary journals. At a later stage, the Connecticut Arts Commission, the New Milford Cultural Commission, and the National Association for Poetry Therapy acknowledged her work as a therapist who uses writing in therapy. In addition to these awards received outside of her country, in 2012 the XV Feria Internacional del Libro paid tribute to Medrano by naming a street from the fairgrounds after her.

Looking at the Village

The personal work and search for an identity, initiated at the end of the eighties, after immigrating to the United States, led Marianela to embark on a foreshadowed journey back to the village, the place of her origins, her traumas, and her wonders.

The village is Copey. It is the borderland of her first childhood, of the stories that featured Indians and Ciguapas as told by her grandfather, and of the Taíno remnants Marianela dug up in the patio of her maternal home.

"In my darkest alcoves, small stalactites formed by archetypes and symbols, grow, and bestow on me the most spectacular landscape that the poem's eye collects," Marianela explains as she attempts to decipher her poetic craft.

Towards the middle of the millennium, Marianela begins a doctorate program in psychology at Sofia University, Palo Alto, California. The poet says that when the moment to choose her dissertation topic came, the topic escaped her until one fall evening, when she went canoeing on one of the rivers along the Connecticut suburban area. Here is where she manifested the topic of her dissertation: Anacaona, the Taína Cacique sentenced to the gallows by Governor Nicolás de Ovando. Anacaona, an invisible and overwhelming presence felt thousands of miles away from her home village.

Can you write an exceptional book of poetry in which 5 goddesses of the Taíno pantheon are in dialogue with the texts of Christopher Columbus and Brother Ramón Pané, while writing a doctoral thesis that aims to demonstrate the influence of Taíno practices on Dominican religious syncretism and how this approach impacts the 32 participants' sense of self and self-esteem?

In Marianela's case, yes, it is possible. *Diosas de la yuca*, published by Torremozas in 2011, written during the arduous process of researching and writing a dissertation, led to much enthusiasm and numerous favorable comments as well as questions from other authors and specialized literary critics. The book's admirers stress its unquestionable poetic quality, the thorough research the author conducted on the Taíno subject matter, the importance of the topic, that is not only limited to the Taíno cosmogony, but also expands to exile, the Caribbean's historical memory, and the problems embedded in urban life these days. The critics, for their part, questioned why a book of poems was being dedicated to the first people on the island known as *Kiskeya* instead of to the Africans brought to the island as slaves, of whom we too are descendants and whose presence is palpable. Marianela addresses this topic in her poem "*El ombligo negro de un bongó*," published in *Regando esencias / The Scent of Waiting* in 1998.

In an interview with the Cuban-Panamanian writer Bessy Reyna, Marianela explains that "cultures do not die but rather transform and adhere themselves to the incoming culture." For that reason, she felt obligated to dedicate her academic and poetic work to the cultural and spiritual practices of the Taínos, who had been pushed aside by the official culture, in order to bring them to the readers' attention. "Our true identity begins when we learn to distinguish between the information we receive and what we really believe in," she wrote in "*La diáspora como experiencia cultural.*"

Prietica, a children's book published by Alfaguara in 2013, followed the publication of *Diosas de la yuca*. Marianela says she delved into children's literature to offer youngsters the stories of Taíno culture that the textbooks provided by the Dominican school system assume is totally extinct.

Converging, Taking Root, Healing, Uprooting

Since 2008, and throughout the decade, Marianela invited writers from different cultures, languages and nationalities to *Confluencia*, a reading series across genres that took place at the Naugatuck Valley Community College in the state of Connecticut. This was a decade in which Marianela continued to be productive as a writer while working as a psychotherapist, serving diverse populations, emphasizing the use of literature as a healing tool, and writing essays for specialized journals; she also organized fashion shows with the GraceWorks Inc. Foundation as a part of her philanthropic work, directed the Palabra Counseling &

Training Center, her own mental health center with establishments in Stamford and New Haven, gave talks on intercultural psychology, writing, conscious eating, and spirituality with an emphasis on the divine feminine for young people and adults in urban and rural communities in India, mature women at a spiritual retreat in New Mexico, and for Dominican psychotherapists in Santo Domingo. In her 2017 presentation on the TED Talks platform titled "A Ciguapa Speaks: On How I Came to Value Wholeness," Marianela begins the story of her journey as a human being, a writer and researcher with a picture of her hometown, Copey.

In 2017, Owlfeather Collective, a publisher that supports quality artists from different cultures, published the bilingual collection *Rooting / Desarraigar: Selected Poems / Poemas seleccionados*, an exquisite personal anthology in English and Spanish. The anthology includes poems from each of Marianela's published books from *Oficio de vivir* to *Prietica*. It is a sensitive and resilient sample of her poetic work, her concerns, her perspectives, her experiences, and everything that has been moving her, taking root and uprooting within and beyond the village. In Marianela's words: "I believe I am mainly moved by passion and a clear vision of the imprint I want to leave behind me in this universe. No matter what I am doing, the poet in me, the writer in me is always taking notes."

Sources

Bidó, Víctor. Book reviews. "*Diosas de la yuca* de Marianela Medrano." Listín Diario. 2018.

Columbié, Ena. "*Diosas de la yuca* de Marianela Medrano." Blog El Exégeta. 2012.

Gómez, Luis Martín. Conversation with Marianela Medrano: "*¿Cómo separarme de lo que me ha llenado tanto?*" Periódico Hoy. Santo Domingo. 2012.

Medrano, Marianela. Fragment from poem "*Jamón y queso.*" Letras salvajes, number 9. 2005.

---. *Oficio de vivir*. Colección Separata. Editora Búho. Santo Domingo, 1986.

---. *Los alegres ojos de la tristeza*. Editora Búho. Santo Domingo. 1987.

---. *Curada de espanto*. Ediciones Torremoza. Madrid, 2002.

---. *Regando esencias / The Scent of Waiting*. Editora Alcance. USA. 1998.

---. "La diáspora como experiencia cultural," essay. *Literatura dominicana en los Estados Unidos / Historia y trayectoria de la diáspora intelectual.* Fundación Global Democracia y Desarrollo. Colección Biblioteca Cultural, Vol. II. Santo Domingo, 2004.

---. *Arte poética*. Authors blog. 2011.

---. *A Ciguapa Speaks: On how I came to value wholeness.* TEDxUrsulineCollege.

---. *Rooting / Desarraigar: Selected Poems/Poemas seleccionados.* Owlfeather Collective. USA, 2017.

---. *Diosas de la yuca.* Ediciones Torremozas. Madrid. 2012.

---. *Prietica.* Alfaguara Infantil. Santo Domingo. 2013.

Moreno, Marisel. *'Burlando la raza': La poesía de escritoras afrodominicanas en la diáspora.* Camino Real. Estudios de las Hispanidades Norteamericanas. Alcalá de Henares: Instituto Franklin. 2011.

Reyna, Bessy. *Conversando con Marianela Medrano.* Identidad Latina / Hispanic Newspaper Connecticut. 2013.

---. *LatinArte News: "Rooting": Nuevo libro bilingüe de Marianela Medrano.* Identidad Latina / Hispanic Newspaper Connecticut. 2018.

POEM BY MARIANELA MEDRANO

Post-Generation X

My son was born in Harlem,
was born in Harlem.
I start to shield my curves
in the train station
where an eye inquires about my behind.

To penis envy add butt envy.

Suffocated phantom
resold in Chinatown for ten dollars.
On to the next case.
The girls, the soft and elastic girls,
interrupt the class for a metaphysical act.
In the room next door, they nurse their infants.
The institutionalized praxis
of the Democrats or the Republicans progresses,
or is it the same old shit?
If not so,
how do you guarantee a generation?
The boys swap girls
according to the climate or the climax.
Isn't this also metaphysics?
My son was born in Harlem, was born in Harlem.
The nurse brought him wrapped in blankets.
He looked like a pastel,
or an imposing gothic structure?
The same one who looks at me and asks for a name,
as if giving birth to him were not enough.
You are me or

I am no longer
as if not being were so easy.
I barely wake up and come with him to Harlem
to cultivate the roses
that the snow has been incubating.
We evoke the future
in the memory of a catalog.
On the sidewalk
laid out on a table
the dresses, the berets.
Africa is also the phantom of a woman
with legs open
half-hidden in the goods peddled by a few vendors.
Will there be enough time to pick up the scraps?
To whom should I give this rosary
if since age fifteen I've known that God is a rip-off?
Earlier, Simone had discovered Medusa's lovely face.
I fall to my knees and dance the dance.
The world is a lone rock
I invent myself in one twist.
Take my son wrapped in blankets
as they showed me in the hospital.
No one will bother with the obsolete
Third World custom of curing navels.
The heart sits in a corner to pulsate.
Later on in kindergarten, the son will come to say
that his mother scribbles poetry,
invents stories,
and the chorus will respond, Who cares?
My son was born in Harlem, was born in Harlem.
Who pays the rent on this new face?
It could have been worse.
It was harder before Vietnam.
Now they come with Welfare under their arms.
Irreversible designs,
indecipherable, the value of X?
My son was born in Harlem,

and it's like setting out without a compass.
Where do I put what I have found, where Silvio?
In a green stomach, black, white, chocolate?
In a nose that's neither flat nor pointy?
My son was born in Harlem, was born in Harlem.
From the gardens the geraniums come up surrealistically.
The value of X?
Uneven shoulder blade in the mysterious Caribbean,
summer of hungry buttocks
dipped in Coca-Cola
and chewing gum.
Christmas with greeting cards
where nothing is missing from the picture
prefigured in the movies.
Or is everything missing?
Who can take this punishment?
Like the grandfather,
I knot coins into the handkerchief.
From them I am smiling on a hill in El Cibao
there where my father's hunger returns,
and the needle sinks in the cry of alarm before the intruder.
My son was born in Harlem, was born...

[*Translated by* Isabel Espinal]

BIOGRAPHY

MARIANELA MEDRANO has been living in Connecticut since 1990. She is a Doctor of Psychology. She frequently offers workshops on poetry / literature and topics related to mental health at different universities and cultural centers in the United States. She has published poetry, narrative, and essays. She directs the reading series *Confluencia* at Naugatuck Valley Community College since 2008.

She has published the following books: *Oficio de vivir* (1986), *Los alegres ojos de la tristeza* (1987), *Regando esencias / The Scent of Waiting* (1998), *Curada de espantos* (2002), *Diosas de la yuca* (2011), *Prietica*, her first children's book (2013), and *Rooting/ Desarraigar* (2017).

"*Generación de Post X*" was published originally in *Regando esencias / The Scent of Waiting* (Ed. Alcance, 1998).

9. SUSSY SANTANA

Shapes of a Kiss

To SUSSY SANTANA
by Rey Andújar

I

That year, the Modern Languages Association (MLA) convention was celebrated in Chicago. On a cold January evening, I sat at the hotel's bar and ordered a beer as I waited for Moira, a friend. There is always something about the first drink of the day. I kept thinking about the young professor from NYU who got upset because I was not more severe when I talked about how the United States left the Caribbean in a state of nuclear abandon. I told the professor that I respected her opinion but did not share it. I am neither an activist nor an academic. I write fiction. So, during events like the MLA, I give presentations to ask myself questions out loud. By the time I started the second beer, Moira finally arrived, accompanied by two very young women.

One of them was the professor from NYU.
Moira introduced me to the professor and the other young woman. They were sisters. The eldest was Luna. She is a guitarist and has her own band. The NYU professor's name was Lía. Her area of specialization was Afro-American writing from the Nixon era.

Lía gave me a kiss and a hug. I ordered a round of drinks for everyone. Almost immediately, I was bombarded with questions. Do you know the Dominican writer Sussy Santana? Of course, I said. My essay about her *Poemas domésticos* is the bomb. I have her novel *Tsunamis Nuclearis* on my reading list. Before I started to complain about all the things we have to read and the little time to do it, the sisters gave me some juicy intel about the famous novel. Sussy didn't write the book. The poet, Águeda Villamán did. Águeda was the ringleader behind the plot to kidnap Mrs. Emma Balaguer. I picked up my jaw from the floor. Who doesn't know about that conspiracy? Not necessarily because her brother, Joaquín "Evil Dwarf" Balaguer was blinded after a bullet was found in his head during the attempted kidnapping, but because that was the same day of the infamous nuclear disaster on the Gulf of Mexico.

I could not believe what I was hearing but I kept my cool. As a fiction writer, you get used to life throwing these asymmetrical hooks at you. Sister Luna went on with the story. She says Águeda was eager to publish that novel. It was her memoir, her life project. She had written all that poetry to find a language that would allow her to relive the past. Publishing it under her own name was impossible because, in the current government, there were Neo-Reformist and Ramfist agents who aimed to wipe out all the remnants of that attack. I asked how Sussy Santana fit in to all of that. The sisters replied, almost at once, that Sussy Santana was none other than Águeda's daughter. *Y como si eso fuera poco*, they also said, "Sussy Santana is our mother."

The story made me switch from beer to rum. There was a quick silence. I was going to say something like, "This is all so surprising," but I remained quiet. Moira compelled me to tell them what I thought about the novel. Luna's dry eyes authorized and encouraged me. Given Sussy's young age, well, I interpreted all of those details about the attack against Balaguer and the nuclear catastrophe that coincidentally took place the same day as a great work of nonfiction. I added that my notes were a bit scattered because I had not read the book in depth. Now, knowing the book was written by Águeda Villamán, and that Sussy and Águeda are connected by a bloodline, well, all of that information inevitably conditions the reading process. I know the novel has also been a big success in Greater Santo Domingo. As I noted this, the professor interrupted me and said, "That's the problem. She went to Greater Santo Domingo for the book presentation, but no one saw her leaving the airport. We haven't heard from her. We are afraid she might have been kidnapped."

Lía, the professor from NYU shot a proposal in my direction. I was the person who was going to rescue their mother. I changed to beer again and broke into laughter because saving people from a nuclear Galrax in the Caribbean is a task for superheroes or something for mutants, perhaps. Well, if you can't rescue her, at least give us news about her. Confirm that she's there. Anything is better than nothing. How had they found out about my future trip to Greater Santo Domingo? She discovered that the Department of Latin-American Studies at the University of Chicago granted me a Chicago Boys Fellowship to do fieldwork in the Caribbean. As part of my research, I was given access to some registered archives in the Galrax basement located in the Columbus Lighthouse, in Greater Santo Domingo. And just like that, with the cards on the table, I realized there was nothing else I could do. I didn't promise them anything. All I said was that I'd be in touch.

II

I travelled to Greater Santo Domingo on a horrible February evening. Outside the terminal, I became sick. The humidity and the smell of tricloxerine burning in the air were too much for my Chicago lungs. Tabar, the escort assigned to me, was waiting outside on a motorpad. I gave him my luggage, took a seat, and concentrated on the road. How futile it was to try to connect my half-memories of la *Hisla* to whatever this is now: Greater Santo Domingo of the Nuclear Redistribution. From time to time, I found Tabar looking at me through the rearview mirror. I pretended to be distracted by the red sea, the water that my ancestors once described as turquoise blue. *Boca Chica, La Caleta, Manresa, Güibia*, names that are now food for historians and a good *nostalsong* to put kids to sleep to after lunch. Oh, to return after so many years to the half-island. Who would've known? We arrived immediately at the nuclear station. The vision of the Galrax at the Columbus Lighthouse was imposing. The young lady that debriefed me was called Tempestad Rizo. She was a curvy white woman with big green eyes. We exchanged some violent looks, or perhaps it was my imagination. The debriefing process really got on my nerves. I had nothing to hide, and the fact that I won the Chicago Boys Fellowship speaks volumes for me, but I guess everybody is the same when dealing with radiation. Once the security check was done, Tabar picked up the passes and we headed to the station's basement. We took a glass elevator from where you could see all the levels of the main reactor. Tabar stopped to get clearance on one floor before arriving at the archives. There was a strange light coming through, so I asked him what it was. Tabar didn't say much but the little he said led me to believe that the Brain Reservoir was behind that light. Yes, exactly. This was the famous lab where they kept the revolutionary brains locked up. If Sussy Santana was in this Galrax, then this was the place to look for her. We arrived at the archives. I plugged my hippocampus to the Hardbox assigned to me. My goal was to evade Tabar's vigilance at some point and then, go and get news of Sussy. It was not hard. I realized the guy liked me, so I shamelessly proposed a kiss. Without thinking twice, he jumped me. I held his body in my arms. He was shaking like a leaf under pouring rain. Can you fall in love with only one little kiss? Yes. A kiss is like a star, so tiny yet so powerful that it can suck up archipelagos like a *Tsunamis Nuclearis*. After the sweet embrace, he let me steal his credentials for the brain reservoir. I have never been a good thief so he noticed everything right away. He didn't understand why I wanted to go to the Brain Reservoir, so I lied and told him I needed some data to give context to my thesis. He authorized me for only fifteen minutes and typed in the password. The doors opened up to the cold air inside. It wasn't difficult to find her. She was in the area of dangerous women writers, among the brains of Aurora Arias and Cartagena Portalatín.

III

Inside a glass rock, connected to thousands of cables and tubes that circulate an amniotic substance, is Sussy Santana, alive, very alive, inside this giant piece of quartz. I carefully moved closer, hooked up my hippocampus, and received all of the hard data in nanoseconds. I felt terribly dizzy as soon as I disconnected my cables. My legs gave out and I fell in front of the central processor unit. I stood up and realized that I was right there in front of the glass rock with her brain inside. My only reaction was to kiss it. Then I felt a surge of power in my heart and brain. All Sussy Santana's files were now mine. They were so great and so many that my hippocampus was about to collapse. Before fainting again, the only thing that I could remember was Tabar, running towards me, brandishing some sort of weapon. I managed to dominate him and to take away the mallet. I damaged the boy but did not kill him. I jumped over his body to hit the glass rock several times until it shattered. This generated a seismogenic force in the reactor. The last thing I remember is Sussy's brain ascending, wrapped in some halo only equal to the singsong of her poetry and the power of her word.

Rey Andújar
Chicago, Fall 2019

POEMS BY SUSSY SANTANA

Paper Dolls

Take us to the slaughterhouse where women are sold
by the pound to the best *reguetonero* and everyone knows
that a woman with no tongue is a village without future
Ratatat, ratatat
Everyone loves wet t-shirts until their daughters are the
    contestants
This morning in Punta Cana a little, very little girl dances and it
    hurts

Rock your nipple to the rhythm, make 'em cry
Rock your nipple to the rhythm, make 'em cry

Take us to the slaughterhouse all made up
because rather dead than simple and we are dead
To make hearts out of guts, without a pulse
To remind us that all vices are born in the kitchen
If I cook like I walk: Watch out

Rock your nipple to the rhythm, make 'em cry
Rock your nipple to the rhythm, make 'em cry

To take us where a gaze turns dreams into nightmares
And words are scissors cutting dolls out of toilette paper,
with Sunday dresses and empty purses

Rock your nipple to the rhythm, make 'em cry
Rock your nipple to the rhythm, make 'em cry

To take us to the slaughterhouse like spies
Where all the meat eaters were raised to the rocking rhythm of the
    nipple
so they wouldn't cry

Femicide

I am disappearing
Silently strangled
I'm ruined
No one kisses me
I'm bruised
The month ends
I'm stitched together
My voice vanishes
I am no more
My children cry out for me
I'm wounded
Am I not worth anything?
I'm demanding
To be seen
To be heard
To be fought for

Blessing

Mami's stomach is full of promises
She left this morning from Santo Domingo to Nicaragua
from Nicaragua to Mexico
from Mexico to San Diego with her passport in her panties
so they could identify her in case she didn't make it
but she has butterflies in her hair
Mami is hungry, but she knows she is going to eat really good if
she holds on a bit longer
She lost her shoes in the sand
Cinderella of the border
Her dress is ruined
Her knees are scarlet
her feet are two loose threads
but she has butterflies in her hair
Mami carries a mountain peak in her eyes
some dogs behind her tracks
a helicopter in the sky
a dark night
a symphony of sobs
her child camping on her breast
but she has butterflies in her hair
Mami left with a group of 20
Mami San Diego
18
Mami I'm almost there
15
Mami helicopter in the air
10
Mami knows she is going to eat real good
5
Mami San Diego
3

Mami

1

Mami reincarnates daily
but she has butterflies in her hair

Woman

Sometimes I am a breadcrumb on the sidewalk
and I die pecked up by birds on the concrete of these
busy streets.

Sometimes I am a terrible joy and I reveal myself through the
 clouds
like a symbol of peace.
Sometimes I am a tent for my daughters
I cover every space and I don't always die when I kill myself.
Sometimes I am a quick and tireless fist
Sometimes I am well-behaved and sensible
or an Almighty BITCH
Sometimes I invent myself in poems and unfamiliar looks.
I am a multiple contradiction,
simply a woman.

BIOGRAPHY

SUSSY SANTANA is a poet. She was born in Santo Domingo in 1976. She is the author of the poetry books *Pelo bueno y otros poemas* (2010) and *Poemas domésticos* (2018), and of the poetry CD *Radio ESL* (2012). Her work has been published in numerous anthologies and cultural magazines. Sussy combines poetry with performance art. Much of her work explores migration, gender and identity. She is the mother of Luna and Lía. Currently, she lives in the United States where, besides writing, she works as an interpreter at the Supreme Court. In 2015, she became the first Latina writer to receive the MacColl Johnson literary fellowship. www.sussysantana.com

"*Muñeca de papel*," "*Feminicidio*," "*Bendición*" and "*Mujer*" are all included in *Poemas domésticos* (Ed. Flora Solar, 2018).

10. ROSA SILVERIO

Rosa Silverio

To ROSA SILVERIO
by Frank Báez

Even though it happened nearly twenty years ago, I remember it like it was yesterday. I was frequenting a literary workshop when, on one occasion, one of the members pulled out a newspaper and read an interview with Rosa Silverio. It was the first time I heard of the poet and narrator from Santiago who—like me—was born in 1978. In the interview she answered questions about her aspirations, influences and concerns regarding a variety of topics. Suddenly, the workshop participants started to criticize her for no apparent reason, making fun of what she was putting forward in the interview in order to disapprove her perspective and ideas. Despite knowing the criticism was unfair and motivated by hate, *machismo*, and elitism, I didn't dare say anything while they vilified her.

In time, I realized they did the same thing with other writers, both men and women, who did not belong to their circle and did not write the way they thought was best. For this reason, I ended up abandoning the workshop. Some years later, when I won a national poetry contest, the same thing that had happened to Rosa Silverio on that occasion happened to me. I was showered by senseless slander, lies, and insults. Literary workshops were no longer necessary by then because the bad vibes came from blogs and social media. What is interesting about this is who stood up for me, armed with all the courage in the world, not caring what she could lose and the friendships she could break; it was Rosa Silverio.

Courage is one quality that characterizes Rosa Silverio. I dare say that it has helped her persist in her literary career. Besides courage, she is tremendously honest and has a unique inner world that anyone can discover in her poems, like spaceships that launch into the dark, the sidereal, and the unknown. She has also published narratives and has edited and coordinated anthologies. She is already acknowledged as one of our most valuable contemporary writers. It is necessary to revisit her work to discover the sensibility that materializes in Dominican literature with the turn of the millennium.

Through the years, Rosa and I have cultivated a lovely friendship. One may think it is impossible to make friends in the literary world. Our persistent friendship, despite her living in Madrid and me in Santo Domingo, is a testimony that proves it is possible.

How did I meet Rosa? The beginning of our friendship is a bit peculiar. It started shortly after I abandoned the literary workshop I mentioned. I really wanted to meet her, so as soon as the opportunity arose, I approached her. It was 1999. We were at the Feria Internacional del Libro in Santo Domingo. It could have been 2000. I can't quite remember. The thing is, it was late, the fair was about to close, and Rosa Silverio had a terrible headache so she needed to get to her brother's house.

"I can take you." I said.

However, there was one detail that complicated everything. Rosa could not remember her brother's address; she only knew he lived in Las Caobas. At that time she was living in Santiago and was hardly familiar with Santo Domingo. I told her to call him, but like me, she did not have her cellular phone on her. Well, everyone knows that poets are known for being distracted. Although, in our defense, I should say that during that time, cellular phones were not as abundant as they are today. Despite all of this, I insisted that she get in the car and lie back in the seat, to get comfortable, since her headache was terrible and she could hardly move. So I stepped on the accelerator and drove towards Las Caobas without really knowing where I was going. Looking back now, I imagine that trip to her brother's house as a metaphor for what happens when one writes poetry. That is, one moves ahead between verses without knowing where one is going until everything is suddenly illuminated, until one recognizes the ground one is stepping on. And of course, one arrives, like that night when I took Rosa to her brother's house. Hence, if there is a way to read Rosa Silverio's poems, it is to let go and dive into the unknown, and I assure you, her verses and words will be the signs and notices that help you find your way back to the house that, at some moment in life, you lost.

POEMS BY ROSA SILVERIO

Crazier Than a Goat

I live between four white walls
hugging my straightjacket
lost in the impenetrable cavities of my mind
attached to Prozac, Trileptal, and Seroquel
running from all the demons of the past
trying to create an aesthetic from the chaos
remaking poetry with my hands
resurrecting every day in the word
I am I was I will be
I attempt to decipher the cosmogony of the world
uncover the god invented by man
create a new theory of myself
become withdrawn, unraveled
find a philosophy
cling on to a theory of science
but my voice is water and it drifts downriver
my voice does not understand of mathematical calculations
nor quantum physics, nor the big bang
nor of any of that which does not fit in my poetics
My voice only lives in madness
and that is where I am and so is the nothingness
me, challenging cosmic accidents
doubting any anthropological revelation
Humanity has no explanation
I am the testimony of an enigma
I am the shadow of which Plato spoke
and this room is my cave
Me in the first-person singular
Me, the invasion, the wheel, the explosion

me, this voluntary reclusion
me, six feet under
me, glued to the ground by an old shoemaker's cement
broken and pulled apart
unstitched
sick
paranoid
borderline
crazier than a goat.

When a Voice Dies

When a voice dies
another comes back to life

A rook flies over my house
the rat has hidden in the kitchen
the knife has cut love in two pieces
and the monster has eaten the most appetizing one

Always, when a voice dies
another comes back to life

A cloth, the detergent, the dark water from the sink
the filth that is wiped up, the hidden secret
the violence that sickens

In this home it has always been winter
the whippings were my children's food
and savagery my obliged daily game

But I have realized:
When a voice dies
another comes back to life

And along came the yearned for night
and my already deformed hand ripped the mandrake
banished the enemy

The sun rose, it's a great day,
the time to love, and as I said:
When a monster dies
a woman comes back to life.

One Must Name This Sadness

One must name this sadness
put a heart on her,
a cat or a snake's eye,
one must put a dress on her
heels
makeup
and take her out
get her drunk
and fuck her in a corner
or in a raunchy motel.
One must beat this sadness,
whip her,
show her who's in charge,
tie her to an electric pole
or pluck off her leaves one evening in September.
One must know that the world
is a spider web or a broad shadow
willing to devour it all,
to swallow everything in a mouthful
or with a swipe.
One must understand that things
have a geographic place, a name,
a specific texture and a shape
and that inside those things
naked and in silence
is sadness,
like a current of cold air
or the sea when the waves have fallen asleep,
like a solitary plot,
a tobacco ranch in the dark
or Matanzas at five o'clock in the evening.
One must know that sadness exists

like the house, the cup of tea,
the clock, the tree, the memories
or the photo of my grandmother
wearing a blouse full of white birds
and whose gaze reminds me of
all of the dead that my poor grandmother
has had to cry.
One must know that sadness not only exists
but she also has a space,
a nook at the center of each thing,
her own coloratura, demands
and even her own schedule
and sometimes one gets tired,
fed up from all the passiveness,
from lying down on the bed,
from taking a jar of pills,
from thinking of ropes, bridges
or in pouring one's heart out,
and all of the sudden one gets up
and says to hell with it
and decides to shift the world's order,
to name sadness,
to label her,
to tell her to fuck off,
and to move on,
always forward,
like on a train
or a *motoconcho*,
even if the void stays where it has always been,
even if nothing is the way it used to be,
even if the dawn is not bright,
even if the sadness never disappears.

BIOGRAPHY

ROSA SILVERIO [Santiago de los Caballeros, 1978]. Journalist and writer. She currently resides in Madrid, Spain. Silverio has published the following poetry books: *De vuelta a casa* (2002), *Desnuda* (2005), *Rosa íntima* (2007), *Arma letal* (2012), *Matar al padre* (2014), *Poemas tristes para días de lluvia* (2016), *Mujer de lámpara encendida* (2016), *Invención de la locura* (2017), *Invenzione della follia* (2018) and the bilingual plaquette *Rotura del tiempo / Broken Time* (2012). She also published the book of stories *A los delincuentes hay que matarlos* (2012). Her stories and poems appear in many anthologies and have been published by magazines and cultural supplements in various countries. Her work has been translated into English, French, Italian, Portuguese and Catalan. She has received several prestigious prizes. Among them are the Premio Nosside de Poesía in Italy, Premio Nacional de Poesía Salomé Ureña, and Premio Letras de Ultramar de Poesía.

"Más loca que una cabra" was published in *Invención de la locura* (Editora Nacional, 2017); *"Cuando una voz muere"* appears in Mujer de lámpara encendida (Huerga & Fierro Editores, 2016); and *"Hay que ponerle nombre a esta tristeza"* was included in *Alma letal* (Editora Nacional, 2011).

COLLABORATORS' BIOGRAPHIES

To all of you and your words, thank you.
Kianny N. Antigua

JOSÉ ACOSTA was born in Santiago, Dominican Republic, in 1964. He is a poet and narrator. He has lived in New York since 1995. He won the Dominican Republic's National Literary Prize on six occasions in the novel, story and poetry genres. In 1994, his book of poems *Territorios extraños* was awarded with the National Poetry Prize, *Salomé Ureña de Henríquez*. In 2003, his book of poems *El evangelio según la Muerte* won the International Poetry Prize *Nicolás Guillén* from Mexico. As a narrator he has received multiple awards, such as the *Premio Nacional de Cuento Universidad Central del Este* for *El efecto dominó* (2000), the National Novel Prize for *Perdidos en Babilonia* (2005) and the National Story Prize for *Los derrotados huyen a París* (2005). In 2015, Acosta won the Casa de las Americas Prize from Cuba for his novel *Un kilómetro de mar*, and he won the National Story Prize with a story called "*El cuento de los bramidos.*" In 2016, he won the National Poetry Prize again for his *Viaje al día venidero*.

CARLOS AGUASACO (Bogotá, 1975). Associate Professor of Latin American cultural studies and Spanish in the Department of Interdisciplinary Studies at The City College of The City University of New York. He has edited ten literary anthologies and published six books of poetry. The most recent are *Poemas del metro de Nueva York* (2014), *Antología de poetas hermafroditas* (2014), *Diente de plomo* (2016), and *Piedra del Guadalquivir* (2017). He also published a short novel and an academic essay on the prime Latin-American superhero, the *Chapulín Colorado: ¡No contaban con mi astucia! México: parodia, nación y sujeto en la* serie de *El Chapulín Colorado* (2014). He is also the editor of *Transatlantic Gazes: Studies on the Historical Links between Spain and North America* (2018). Carlos is the founder and director of Artepoética Press (artepoetica.com), a publisher specializing in Hispanic authors and topics. In addition, he is the director of The Americas Film Festival of New York (taffny.com). Carlos has co-organized conferences and international symposiums with institutions such as the Franklin Institute (Universidad de Alcalá), the Cervantes Institute, the Transatlantic Project (Brown University) and the Universidad Tres de Febrero, among others. His poems have been translated into English, French, Portuguese, Romanian, Galician and Arabic. Web: carlosaguasaco.com

REY ANDÚJAR (Santo Domingo, 1978) Author of several novels and collections of stories, such as *El hombre triángulo* (Isla Negra Editores) and *Candela* (Alfaguara) which was selected as one of the best novels of 2009 by the PEN Club of Puerto Rico and it was adapted into film by Andrés Farías Cintrón. The stories from *Amoricidio* received the *Premio de Cuento Joven* awarded by Feria del Libro in 2007, and his collection of stories *Saturnario* won the *Premio Letras de Ultramar* in 2010. His novel *Los gestos inútiles* won the *IV Premio Alba de Narrativa Latinoamericana y Caribeña* at the Feria del Libro in Havana (2015). He writes for film, theater, and holds a Doctorate in Philosophy and Caribbean Literature from the Centro de Estudios Avanzados de Puerto Rico y el Caribe. He is a humanities professor at Governors State University in Chicago.

AURORA ARIAS Dominican poet and narrator. Arias has published two books of poetry, *Vivienda de pájaro* and *Piano lila*. She has published three books of stories, *Invi Paradise, Fin de mundo*, and *Emoticons*. Her poems and stories have been translated into English, French, German, Icelandic, Bengali, and Italian, and have been selected by different anthologies such as *Common Threads: Afro Hispanic Women's Literature* (USA, 1998),

Sólo cuento (Mexico, 2010), *Les bonnes nouvelles de l'Amérique latine* (Francia, 2011), *Un lugar en la memoria: Relatos de dictaduras en América Latina* (Argentina, 2016), *Indómita y brava: Antología de poetas dominicanos contemporáneos* (Spain, 2017), and *No creo que yo esté aquí de más, Antología poética* (Spain, 2018). Currently, she lives in the United States where she carries out workshops and other literary activities.

FRANK BÁEZ born in Santo Domingo in 1978. He is a poet, a narrator and a chronicler. His latest publications: *Este es el futuro que estabas esperando* (Seix Barral, 2017), and *Llegó el fin del mundo a mi barrio* (Sonámbulos Ediciones, 2019).

CÉSAR SÁNCHEZ BERAS Lawyer, poet, playwright and schoolteacher. Graduate of the Universidad Autónoma de Santo Domingo. He studied pedagogy and literature at Framinghan State College. He has engaged in cultural management. His works for children have been read and performed in the Dominican Republic and the United States where they form part of school reading curriculums. He has won prizes as a poet, a children's literature writer and a playwright. In 2004 and 2014, he won the *Premio Anual de Poesía* and the *Premio Anual de Literatura Infantil*. He has received three national prizes for *décimas* (ten-line stanzas), the *Premio de Poesía UCE* and the *Premio de Poesía Alianza Cibaeña*.

KEISELIM A. MONTÁS (Santo Domingo, Dominican Republic, 1968) has lived in the United States since 1985, where he completed a bachelor's and a master's degree in Spanish language and Literature. He has published poems, stories and essays; his work has been included in anthologies and magazines, and has been acknowledged by literary competitions. He is founder and editor of the small independent publisher, *Élitro Editorial del Proyecto Zompopos*.

OSIRIS MOSQUEA was born in San Francisco de Macorís, Dominican Republic. She attended the Universidad Autónoma de Santo Domingo (U.A.S.D.) where she earned a Bachelor of Arts in accounting. She holds a Master of Arts in Spanish Language and Literature from the City College of New York. Mosquea is a poet and narrator. She is a founding member of *Trazarte Huellas Creativas* in New York City and coeditor of *Revista Trazos*. Her work has been published in magazines, newspapers and anthologies in the United States and other parts of the world: *Antología Poética Terre de Poétes Terre de Paix* (Paris, 2007); *Un poema a Pablo Neruda, Isla Negra* (Santiago de Chile, 2010); *Antología del XIV Encuentro Internacional de Poetas en Zamora* (Michoacan, 2010); *Noches de vino y rosas. La antología* (New York, 2010); *Mujeres de palabra; Poética y antología* (New York, 2010); *Nostalgias de arena* (Santo Domingo, 2011). Her poetry publications include: *Una mujer: Todas las mujeres* (miCielo ediciones, Mexico, 2015); *Viandante en Nueva York* (Artepoética Press, New York, 2013); and *Raga del tiempo* (Santo Domingo, 2009). As a narrator, she published *De segunda mano* (Books & Smith, New York, 2018).

NÉSTOR E. RODRÍGUEZ (La Romana, Dominican Republic, 1971). He is a professor of Latin American Literature at the University of Toronto. He published *Escrituras de desencuentro en la República Dominicana* (Mexico City, 2005), this study was awarded the *Premio al Pensamiento Caribeño* in Mexico in 2004; *La isla y su envés* (San Juan, 2003) which received the *Premio Concha Meléndez de Crítica Literaria* in Puerto Rico, and *Crítica para tiempos de poco fervor* (Santo Domingo, 2009). As a poet, he published *Animal pedestre* (San Juan, 2004), *El desasido* (Mexico City, 2009), *Limo* (Rio de Janeiro, 2018) and *Poesía reunida* (Santo Domingo, 2018).

COMPILER & EDITOR

KIANNY N. ANTIGUA (San Francisco de Macorís, Dominican Republic, 1979). Narrator, poet and translator. Kianny is a Senior Lecturer at Dartmouth College, and works as a translator and adopter for Pepsqually VO & Sound Design Inc. She has published twenty-two children's books, four of short stories, two of poetry, a journal, and a book of microfiction. In 2018, she won the International Latino Book Award for her bilingual book *Greña / Crazy Hair* for Most Inspirational Children's Picture Book. She won the *Premio Letras de Ultramar* under the children's literature category twice, in 2015 and 2017. In 2016, she won the *XV Concurso Nacional de Cuento Sociedad Cultural Alianza Cibaeña*. In the same year, she was the honored writer of the *XIII Feria del Libro de Escritoras Dominicanas* (NY). In addition, she has won sixteen more literary prizes in both the Dominican Republic and the United States. Her work can be found in several anthologies, textbooks, literary journals, newspapers, and other platforms. Also, some of her short stories have been translated into Italian, French and English.

TRANSLATOR

KADIRI VAQUER FERNÁNDEZ (Puerto Rico, 1987). Kadiri is a Puerto Rican poet, translator and professor. She holds a B.A. in Interdisciplinary Studies from the University of Puerto Rico, a M.F.A. in Creative Writing in Spanish from New York University, and a Ph.D. in Spanish with a minor in Portuguese from Vanderbilt University. She has published two books of poetry, *Andamiaje* (Ediciones Callejón, 2013) and *Ritos de Pasaje* (La Secta de los Perros, 2019). Her work has been published in anthologies and several online magazines. She has translated fiction, non-fiction, and poetry.

www.ingramcontent.com/pod-product-compliance
Lightning Source LLC
LaVergne TN
LVHW011837060526
838200LV00053B/4071